Deconstruction of Natural Order
The Legacy of the Russian Revolution

RUSSIA
Yesterday, today and tomorrow
Politics — Culture — Economy — Religion

Editors: Joachim Diec, Anna Jach, Michał Kuryłowicz

Vol. 23

Deconstruction of Natural Order
The Legacy of the Russian Revolution

edited by Joachim Diec

Kraków

Review
prof. dr hab. Roman Bäcker

Copy editing
Joanna Hałaczkiewicz

Cover design
Anna Słota

ISBN 978-83-7638-904-2
DOI: 10.12797/9788376389042

Publication financed by
Faculty of International and Political Studies,
Jagiellonian University in Kraków

KSIĘGARNIA AKADEMICKA
ul. św. Anny 6, 31-008 Kraków
tel./faks: 12 431 27 43, 12 421 13 87
e-mail: akademicka@akademicka.pl

Księgarnia internetowa:
www.akademicka.pl

Contents

Chapter 5

DOI: 10.12797/9788376389042.01

JOACHIM DIEC ⓘD https://orcid.org/0000-0002-3335-3772

Introduction
Natural Order and the Revolution

The Russian Revolution of 1917 came as a surprise not only to millions of Russians but also to the elites in the rest of the world. Few scholars, politicians and historians both in Russia and abroad had suspected that the highly conservative and rural country could overtake the Western powers on their way to economic egalitarianism. In fact, there was a precedent seven years before: the Mexican Revolution. The main problem, however, was not in Russia's lack of readiness but in the fact that after the tragic events of 1917 the state seemed to have completely changed its own system of values.

Russia under the old regime can be described as an empire: a kind of state which is neither completely national nor completely universal. Upon establishing the Russian Empire in 1721, Peter the Great could not draw a clear definition of the new political being. However, one has to remember that the vast plains east of Poland underwent essential rather than accidental changes several times before the Russian empire was officially established. Before 862, according to the *Primary Chronicle*, it was a badly organized collection of East Slavic settlements. Then it began to be ruled by a Scandinavian elite, gaining the new Germanic name – Rus', and becoming a semi-military organization economically based on several burghs and on the route toward the Black Sea. The next step was taken by Prince Volodimir the Great, who decided to baptize himself and his people according to the Byzantine rite tradition. The East Christian (after 1054 – Orthodox) Old Rus', whose main center moved from Novgorod to Kiev, broke apart after the death of Yaroslav the Wise, a brilliant ruler, and the capital moved again – to Vladimir on Klazma (*Primary Chronicle*, transl. of 1953).

At the end of the 1230s, the municipalities were invaded by Batu-Khan, the leader of the Mongol Western (Golden) Horde. After that, the East of historical Rus' was subordinated to the despotic leadership of the Golden Horde and was permeated with the Mongol principles of militarism, centralism and absolute monarchy where the will of the leader was the only source of law. However, the Orthodox church was an exception: it enjoyed relative respect and was in no way affected by the despotic Crimean state. The situation was different in the western part of the old Kievan domain, which was liberated from the Mongol hegemony and annexed by the Grand Duchy of Lithuania and (in the case of Galicia) by Poland.

When in the 15th century Moscow became the leading power in the area controlled by the Horde, the Grand Duchy of Moscow, which in 1547, thanks to the ambitions of Ivan the Terrible, was named Tsardom of All Rus', adopted some essential Mongol political standards, but at the same time it cultivated the myth of the Third Rome – the bedrock of the only true faith. Moscow was different from the Catholic and Protestant West and glorified its own uniqueness (as emphasized by the German emperor's envoy, Herberstein, 1557).

At the beginning of the age of Enlightenment, Peter the Great dispelled the myth of the unique Orthodox domain and began to construct a new state – the Russian Empire, which was supposed to become one of the leading European powers. The mission of the state was in the state itself: the Tsar, who was now officially titled

Emperor, exercised all key prerogatives, even the ones that referred to the church since the institution of patriarchy was abolished.

A short review was provided to illustrate the fact that the Russian state changed its origin myth several times. As it was expressed by Petr Chaadaev, the founder of Russian intellectual westernism, in his famous *First Philosophical Letter*, Russia has no history – it has built its own civilization from scratch several times:

> Our memories reach back no further than yesterday; we are, as it were, strangers to ourselves. We move through time in such a singular manner that, as we advance, the past is lost to us forever. That is but a natural consequence of a culture that consists entirely of imports and imitation. Among us there is no internal development, no natural progress; new ideas sweep out the old, because they are not derived from the old but tumble down upon us from who knows where. We absorb all our ideas ready-made, and therefore the indelible trace left in the mind by a progressive movement of ideas, which gives it strength, does not shape our intellect. We grow, but we do not mature; we move, but along a crooked path, that is, one that does not lead to the desired goal. We are like children who have not been taught to think for themselves: when they become adults, they have nothing of their own – all their knowledge is on the surface of their being, their soul is not within them. That is precisely our situation.
>
> Peoples, like individuals, are moral beings. Their education takes centuries, as it takes years for that of persons. In a way, one could say that we are an exception among peoples. We are one of those nations, which do not seem to be an integral part of the human race, but exist only in order to teach some great lesson to the world (Chaadaev, 1829).

Does that mean that the Russian Revolution of 1917 should not be treated as a disaster and at the same time something extraordinary in the history of the great country? The answer is not easy since the essence of the problem lies in the criteria one could apply for the analysis. In the same way as it was after the Petrine Reforms, the conservatives (national traditionalists), such as the Slavophiles, tried to emphasize the fact that the radical change humiliated the nation and acted against its spiritual essence (Alschen, 2013, p. 26). After the revolution of 1917, countless thinkers complained about the violation of Russian values: nationalists such as Ivan Ilyin, Christian philosophers with Nikolai Berdyaev, Sergei Bulgakov and Petr Struve at the helm, the liberal camp headed by Pavel Milyukov and even revolutionary socialists such as Victor Chernov criticized and demonized Lenin (Чернов, 1924).

The main objective of this book results from the dilemma of total change and is to determine at least some of the essential characteristics of the Russian Revolution that reveal themselves in some closer and further consequences. This means that one of the basic assumptions of the book is that it is possible to trace old mental constructions in contemporary processes even though, as it was mentioned above, Russia has a strong inclination toward total annihilation of former formulas.

The first task was to draw a comprehensive image of the new legal principles that underlay the revolutionary reforms. This way, in Chapter 1, we try to reconstruct the Bolshevik understanding of law and state, which became the obligatory set of norms for several generations of people who spent most of their lives under the communist rule.

Chapter 2 briefly analyzes the relation between state, business and society before and after the revolution of 1917. The intention of the text is to point out the traditional forms of the relation and the new, unexpected ones, which lead to different practical results. We assume that the mechanisms worked out in the times of Witte and Stolypin were in fact deconstructed or even totally negated in the following years, which led to various kinds of socio-economic disaster. That is why the Russian state has to seek new forms of public and economic management with the main imperatives of democratic incentive and economic effectiveness.

The next two chapters focus on questions concerning selected problems which affected Russia after the collapse of the USSR. One of them refers to Russia's foreign policy – to the secessions in the post-Soviet area, which are treated as consequences of an odd interpretation of international law. The purpose of the chapter is to analyze the Russian elite's attitude to the customary, relatively established norms that underlie the world order and to provide material for conclusions about the revolutionary legacy as an explanatory factor for aggressive international behaviors.

Chapter 4, which refers to contemporary processes, is nominally about something that has not happened: a hypothetical, potential revolution which is supposed to introduce another paradigm of the Russian state. We ask the question about the probability of a nationalist revolt in Russia, which was proclaimed by many thinkers but never realized by the angry people. We thus suggest that Russia's present-day identity is somewhat unclear and that a search for another origin myth makes sense.

Last but not least, looking for the core of revolutionary thinking, we would like to present a study of political gnosis which underlies many radical changes. Gnostic thinking has always been based on axiological oppositions: equality and inequality, progressivity and reaction, paving the road to violence in the name of the light side of the Force. This way we try to suggest that the gnostic paradigm can be an efficient explanatory device for the description of a revolutionary mentality.

Those who accuse the revolutionary thinking of being responsible for particular crimes as well as for social and spiritual destruction in general usually emphasize the violation of "naturalness". Revolutions are charged with the imposition of artificial and harmful intellectual simplifications which are opposed to the spontaneous and natural order of things. The understanding of natural order, however, has varied throughout centuries and depended mainly on the ideological position of theoreticians. The notion of natural order is related to the concept of natural law, which has been explored in philosophical and theological doctrines several times. We understand **natural order as a state of beings (including humans) that allows them to behave according to** *natural law* **without restrictions**. The scope of these two notions may include various areas; in our book they refer to the social, political and economic spheres of the state.

Natural law is not necessarily equal to *the state of nature*, which we understand as a spontaneous outcome of the functioning of nature (even if "nature" refers to the functioning of humans). This term usually refers to the pre-social or pre-civilizational state of mankind, to a theoretical rather than historical wilderness. If we look at the most customary understanding of natural law, we realize that it is generally depicted as a set of principles that lead people to goodness. This concept of natural law was initiated by classical Greek philosophers such as Empedocles, Plato and Aristotle, who is usually treated as the philosopher who formulated the problem in the most complete form in the ancient times (Aristotle, 1998, p. 58). The concept of natural law was in a way tackled in *Genesis*, in the description of Cain's sin and in Abraham's hesitation about God's intentions concerning Sodom (Genesis, 18,25), and by St. Paul in his *Epistle to Romans* (Romans, 2, 14–15). Natural law was treated with proper attention by the Fathers, including St. Augustine, and by medieval thinkers, including St. Thomas Aquinas, who claimed that it is because of *natural law* that rational beings can participate in *eternal law*. Since the latter is not entirely intelligible for imperfect humans, they have to resort to *Divine Law*, which is given by God to save people from errors and eternal condemnation (Aquinas, Summa Theologica, I–II, qq. 90–106). The authority of natural law also lies behind Locke's *Second Treatise on Government*, which elaborates on basic human rights rather than obligations.

If we consider the topic of the state of nature, the vision might not be that optimistic because the understanding of nature is not necessarily associated with rights; it can also be comprehended as the perceived world of living organisms. One of the oldest concepts of naturalness comes from Hobbes, whose vision of the nature of man seems quite pessimistic:

So that in the nature of man, we find three principall causes of quarrel. First, Competition; Secondly, Diffidence; Thirdly, Glory. The first, maketh men invade for Gain; the second, for Safety; and the third, for Reputation. The first use Violence, to make themselves Masters of other mens persons, wives, children, and cattell; the second, to defend them; the third, for trifles, as a word, a smile, a different opinion, and any other signe of undervalue, either direct in their Persons, or by reflexion in their Kindred, their Friends, their Nation, their Profession, or their Name.

There Is Always Warre Of Every One Against Every One Hereby it is manifest, that during the time men live without a common Power to keep them all in awe, they are in that condition which is called Warre; and such a warre, as is of every man, against every man. For WARRE, consisteth not in Battell onely, or the act of fighting; but in a tract of time, wherein the Will to contend by Battell is sufficiently known: and therefore the notion of Time, is to be considered in the nature of Warre; as it is in the nature of Weather. For as the nature of Foule weather, lyeth not in a showre or two of rain; but in an inclination thereto of many dayes together: So the nature of War, consisteth not in actuall fighting; but in the known disposition thereto, during all the time there is no assurance to the contrary. All other time is PEACE.

Whatsoever therefore is consequent to a time of Warre, where every man is Enemy to every man; the same is consequent to the time, wherein men live without other security, than what their own strength, and their own invention shall furnish them withall. In such condition, there is no place for Industry; because the fruit thereof is uncertain; and consequently no Culture of the Earth; no Navigation, nor use of the commodities that may be imported by

Sea; no comimodious Building; no Instruments of moving, and removing such things as require much force; no Knowledge of the face of the Earth; no account of Time; no Arts; no Letters; no Society; and which is worst of all, continuall feare, and danger of violent death; And the life of man, solitary, poore, nasty, brutish, and short (Hobbes, 1651, ch. 13).

The state of nature depicted in such a way seems to be an obstacle rather than a proper environment for human activity. In other words, the natural man cannot put up with the state of nature, which is described as *bellum omnium contra omnes* and interferes with the divine commandment to be fruitful and multiply. This way we realize that natural law (as the emanation of eternal law), which is an intelligible structure of moral goodness and prosperity, takes people away from the state of nature and locates the source of naturalness in another order. It is not necessarily true that Locke's treatise provides a polemic narrative against Hobbes; it is rather a tale about another kind of nature, one which is able to overcome terrestrial physical inequality and subordinate all men to a law that is in a way perceived in one's life experience but does not refer to the physical world. What both Hobbes and Locke aimed at is the liberation from spontaneous brutality and the construction of the "state of predictability", which is entirely different from the *state of nature*. The latter is structurally expressed in social Darwinism, where the death of the weak is perceived as natural and even advisable for developing species.

The notion of natural order is also associated with some other understandings. In some concepts, natural order is artistic: art may create forms which either reflect higher "natural" harmony or distort it. Even within the blurry category of art one can realize that people as social beings tend to invoke a higher order which is supposed to be natural in a non-physical sense of *naturalness*.

In the tradition of economic liberalism, naturalness and natural order refer to the wealth of nations, which is supposed to grow only if the authorities open the state's economy to the power of the invisible hand of the free market. The classical principle of no governmental support and no barriers, which was suggested by Adam Smith, was later expressed in some other incarnations of liberalism including the works of Friedrich von Hayek. Hayek makes a distinction between two kinds of order. One of them

> is achieved by *arranging* the relations between the parts according to a preconceived plan we call in the social field an *organization*. The extent to which the power of many men can be increased by such deliberate co-ordination of their efforts is well-known and many of the achievements of man rest on the use of this technique.

The other one

> ...which is characteristic not only of biological organisms (to which the originally much wider meaning of the term organism is now usually confined), is an order which is not made by anybody but which forms itself. It is for this reason usually called a "spontaneous" or sometimes (for reasons we shall yet explain) a 'polycentric' order. If we understand the forces which determine such an order, we can use them by creating the conditions under which such an order will form itself (Hayek, 1981).

As a matter of fact, Hayek's understanding of natural order in economy still sticks to the Darwinian scheme since the state of naturalness in the circumstances of a free market is unpredictable. The libertarian concepts (such as the one of Robert Nozick) do not add anything important to this narrative apart from the idea of the minimum state. It seems, however, that a deeper understanding of the question has been proposed by Hans-Hermann Hoppe, who criticizes democracy (as opposed to monarchy) because of its natural inclination to promote elites that lack basic moral values. A truly democratic elite is a bunch of expropriators who in the long run are unable to foster production. That is why a "private government" seems more productive:

The defining characteristic of private government ownership is that the expropriated resources and the monopoly privilege of future expropriation are individually owned. The appropriated resources are added to the ruler's private estate and treated as if they were a part of it, and the monopoly privilege of future expropriation is attached as a title to this In contrast, with a publicly owned government the control over the government apparatus lies in the hands of a trustee, or caretaker. The caretaker may use the apparatus to his personal advantage, but he does not own it. He cannot sell government resources and privately pocket the receipts, nor can he pass government possessions onto his personal heir. He owns the current use of government resources, but not their capital value. Moreover, while entrance into the position of a private owner of government is restricted by the owner's personal discretion, entrance into the position of a caretaker-ruler is open. Anyone, in principle, can become the government's caretaker.

From these assumptions two central, interrelated predictions can be deduced: (1) A private government owner will tend to have a systematically longer planning horizon, i.e., his degree of time preference will be lower, and accordingly, his degree of economic exploitation will tend to be less than that of a government caretaker; and (2), subject to a higher degree of exploitation the nongovernmental public will also be comparatively more present--oriented under a system of publicly owned government than under a regime of private government ownership. (1) A private government owner will predictably try to maximize his total wealth; i.e., the present value of his estate and his current income. He will not want to increase his current income at the expense of a more than proportional drop in the present value of his assets, and because acts of current income acquisition invariably have repercussions on present asset values (reflecting the value of all future-expected--asset earnings discounted by the rate of time preference), private ownership in and of itself leads to economic calculation and thus promotes farsightedness.

In the case of the private ownership of government, this implies a distinct moderation with respect to the ruler's incentive to exploit his monopoly privilege of expropriation, for acts of expropriation are by their nature parasitic upon prior acts of production on the part of the nongovernmental public. Where nothing has first been produced, nothing can be expropriated; and where everything is expropriated, all future production will come to a shrieking halt (Hoppe, 2001, pp. 45–46).

Upon examining the history of Russia in the early decades of the 20th century, one may come to the realization that the Hoppean scheme describes the situation of Russia's society and economy. Before the beginning of WW1, the growth of production in this country was in almost all sectors one of the fastest in Europe. The legal regulations in Russia's absolute monarchy provided sufficient stability for investors and capital could be accumulated in an atmosphere of security. The revolution, which was an outcome of the highly destructive war, abolished these conditions and led to an economic and social disaster, especially during the time of War Communism. Russia became subject to a totalitarian experiment, where expropriation became the principle of new justice: "rob what has been robbed" (see brilliant descriptions of the process in Wolfe (1969) and Lohr (2003)).

What has to be emphasized, however, is the fact that the idea of expropriation cannot be separated from the problem of social stratification. The red camp – the Bolsheviks – and, in the "soft" version, the democratic leftists such as the Mensheviks or the Socialist Revolutionaries, proclaimed far-reaching egalitarianism. Its range stretched from the abolition of private property of land to the nationalization of industry and banks. This way the new authorities got rid of the old economic elite, which had been formed over decades (or even centuries), but in the other spheres the situation was by no means better: most of the Orthodox clergymen were either shot on the spot or placed in labor camps, white officers who did not manage to escape had to account for being shot (if they were lucky enough to avoid torture), most academic and high school teachers, lawyers etc. had to escape from Russia to become cabbies or janitors in Western Europe or put up with gradual marginalization and, in the Stalin era, with ultimate physical liquidation, which usually involved a long and "active" interrogation.

This way the new incarnation of Russia – the Soviet Union – had to be conducted by its new elite, which was nominally "democratic" in the sense that it tried to appreciate "the people". The new leaders were originally recruited from the Bolshevik Party, VKP(b), which was a collection of radical leftists who generally belonged to the margin of the imperial society. The most prominent ones were either entirely uprooted or had dark biographies like Stalin, the leading expropriator and experienced murderer, who earned money for the party by robbing banks (Sebag Montefiore, 2007). The dramatic events that took place in 1917 and in the following years formed a dysfunctional system which was supposed to be a negation of both absolute monarchy and liberal democracy. The new regime tried to disqualify the tyranny based on the domination of one person and the ideological superstructure of the Orthodox faith combined with the imaginary pressure of Great Russian chauvinism. It also refuted the liberal dreams which, as they believed, led to appalling social inequality and to the establishment of the bourgeoisie – a parasitic false elite that deterred the proletariat from genuine development. These convictions not only led to such things as the physical liquidation of the liberal and socialist opposition as well as the imperial family, but they also wiped out the institution of private property.

The Bolsheviks and a number of useful idiots in the West, according to the principles of Marxism, believed that the experiment may open new opportunities to the development of humanity and become an alternative to the older systemic solutions. However, as it was emphasized by Hoppe, the search for a more humane order (i.e. one that incites positive development) may consist in something entirely different. The legitimacy of monarchical rule "appears to have been irretrievably lost" but

> ...at the same time, and still more importantly, a positive alternative to monarchy and democracy – the idea of a natural order – must be delineated and understood. On the one hand, this involves the recognition that it is not exploitation, either monarchical or democratic, but private property, production, and voluntary exchange that are the ultimate sources of human civilization. On the other hand, it involves the recognition of a fundamental sociological insight (which incidentally also helps identify precisely where the historic opposition to monarchy went wrong): that the maintenance and preservation of a private property based exchange economy requires as its sociological presupposition the existence of a voluntarily acknowledged natural elite – a *nobilitas naturalis*.
>
> The natural outcome of the voluntary transactions between various private property owners is decidedly non-egalitarian, hierarchical, and elitist. As the result of widely diverse human talents, in every society of any degree of complexity a few individuals quickly acquire the status of an elite. Owing to superior achievements of wealth, wisdom, bravery or a combination thereof, some individuals come to possess "natural authority," and their opinions and judgments enjoy widespread respect. Moreover, because of selective mating and marriage and the laws of civil and genetic inheritance, positions of natural authority are more likely than not passed on within a few noble families. It is to the heads of these families with long-established records of superior achievement, farsightedness, and exemplary personal conduct that men turn with their conflicts and complaints against each other, and it is these very leaders of the natural elite who typically act as judges and peacemakers, often free of charge, out of a sense of obligation required and expected of a person of authority or even out of a principled concern for civil justice, as a privately produced "public good" (Hoppe, 2001, p. 71).

To conclude, we realize that such a concept of natural order provokes several questions referring to the legacy of the Russian Revolution, which broke out to boost the self-esteem of the

Russian people. First of all, we are entitled to ask about the *nature of unnaturalness*, which is supposed to be the core of social evil. Next, we also have to explore the issue of *equality*: the problem of *the people* and of *the elite* in the context of revolutionary ideas and events. Another issue lies in the relation between the *revolution* and the *natural order*, which is the basic question of our book. Last but not least, we also have to examine the Russian Revolution in the context of natural order from the pragmatic perspective. In other words, we assume that the unclear intuition of *naturalness* in the spheres of politics (both internal and international), economy and social life reveals itself in the commonly perceived and mathematically articulated prosperity and security.

DOI: 10.12797/9788376389042.02

ADAM BOSIACKI* (iD) https://orcid.org/0000-0001-6455-0632
University of Warsaw

Chapter 1

Shaping the First Totalitarian State

The Political and Legal System at the Beginning
of the Russian Revolution (October 1917–1921)
and its Implications

This chapter describes the first concepts of law and the political system under the Bolshevik rule[1]. Obviously and paradoxically, these concepts have not been studied so far for several reasons.

The first reason is the almost complete absence of materials, sources of knowledge about the law of the studied period. Many Soviet lawyers and political analysts writing in those years continued their work also after the end of the war communism era, yet they often changed their previous stance for a variety of reasons. Hence, their earlier ideas have often remained almost completely unknown.

---

* Prof. dr hab., University of Warsaw, Faculty of Law and Administration.
[1]   To some extent the present text refers to the author's monograph (Bosiacki, 2012).

Another reason is the total change in the legal ideology of the Bolshevik state at the end of the described period. In 1922, a completely new legal system was introduced: the unwritten law was replaced by a new one. First of all, under the New Economic Policy (NEP) the institution of civil law as a whole was reintroduced; in this way the institution of property law, a civil code, was developed. This implied, among other things, the reintroduction of civil rights (to a limited extent). In this sense, the legal system of the RSFSR (Russian Soviet Federal Socialist Republic) after 1922 was a total negation of the earlier legal concepts. This does not mean, however, that the previously developed system, or more precisely a number of conceptions of war communism in Bolshevik Russia, were not transferred into the legislation of the subsequent period. Conversely, the concepts of civil war law were widely introduced not only into the Soviet Union's legal system of the 1920s and the Stalinist period, but also into the legal systems of other communist countries under Soviet influence after World War II. Some of the institutions born in Lenin's country continue to exist within the Polish law until now. There is also no question about the fact that the model of a state, society and law which was specific for the entire Soviet-style communist system was developed in Soviet Russia during the period of war communism. In this sense, the Bolshevik concept of the state and the normative order was the first totalitarian conception of the Soviet system. It was also the first model of a totalitarian state existing in reality in the 20th century.

The present work uses nearly all the legal literature of the Bolshevik state written between the years 1917–1921, which was sometimes scarcely available. The author analyzed periodicals and books published in that period (over 600 titles). He also succeeded in gaining access to the archival materials from the Central State Archive of the Russian Federation (former Central State Archive of the October Revolution) and the collections of the St. Petersburg

Museum of History. Using the documents of the former USSR Ministry of Transport and family archives, the author studied the life and career of one of the most outstanding Soviet experts in civil law, Alexander Grigorevich Goikhbarg (1883–1962), whose ideas were spread not only to the real socialism countries but also, to some extent, to other countries.

Owing to the archival materials, the author was able to obtain unpublished information and data on the Bolshevik science of law, their work on designing the first Soviet constitution (July 1918), the work of the revolutionary tribunals, the People's Commissariat of Justice, the Cheka and, finally, biographical materials of the leading lawyers of the period.

The work was preceded by a kind of prelude consisting in an analysis of Lenin's viewpoint on the law before the October Revolution[2] in connection with the still surviving number of myths and oversimplified opinions about the Bolshevik leader. We know that Lenin, an educated lawyer, was somehow connected with the profession of a barrister. As a charismatic leader, he was the father and sole leader of the Bolshevik party, an organism resembling a conspiratorial organization rather than a political party and maybe for this reason called by him a party of a new type.

An analysis of Lenin's writings justifies the conclusion that he had never written about law and that he never presented any consistent view on this subject. The Bolshevik leader's practice as an attorney was rather unimpressive (also during his university years). The subject of law does not exist as his point of interest in the subsequent editions of all his works. This is not a coincidence. The term "law" was used relatively seldom in the Soviet Union after the early 1930s and it was replaced by the word закон meaning the Act of Law. This was, of course, in tune with the Marxist and Leninist understanding of what law actually is.

---

[2] A separate investigation on this subject was published in Bosiacki (1997).

Lenin's attitude towards law, however, was somewhat more in-
-depth. Being a Marxist, the Bolshevik leader very soon (in 1894,
that is, at the age of 24) adopted the thesis that law is the will of the
ruling class and is shaped by this class to serve its own interests
which are opposite to the interests of the other social classes
(Lenin, 1983, pp. 120–121). In this construction, law is always
a variable category; it is shaped by the ruler (class rule).

In the quoted article, Lenin (1983) described (in an indirect
way, as can be observed above) his attitude toward law as the
"critical revision of the Hegelian philosophy of law" consistent
with the spirit of Marxism. More interestingly, however, a peculiar
"product of the era" was Lenin's linking of the Marxist idea of law
with Russian "legal nihilism"[3], popular in the country at the turn
of the centuries. The synthesis of these ways of thinking led to the
conviction that law as a social phenomenon was an instrument of
the struggle of classes and, being the expression of the will of the
ruling class, it could not limit this will in any way. Lenin had all his
life believed that law performed first of all the repressive function
and was eagerly identified with the unwritten law.[4]

At least several passages from Lenin's works written in the pre-
revolution years can be cited to support this view. For example,
an expert in this subject, Andrzej Walicki, quotes the Leninist
definition of the "dictatorship of the proletariat" in his description
of the Leninist system:

> The scientific conception of dictatorship means nothing else but
> power not limited by anything, unrestricted by any laws, any rules
> what so ever, any regulations, and relying directly on violence
> (Walicki, 1995, p. 104).

---

[3]　This term generally meant the conviction that written law could not reflect
the eternal and universal legal ideas: justice, good, and even beauty. As time
passed, this attitude led to the *tradition of criticizing the law*. Comp. e.g. Walicki
(1995, pp. 17–114).

[4]　A similar opinion was first presented in Bosiacki (1997, p. 42).

Lenin had (marginally) voiced similar views more than once before the revolution. He kept saying that the regulations of the constitution (Lenin, 1986a, p. 327), "all questions of law--abidingness" (Lenin, 1987a, p. 200) and the existence of law as a general question "independent of the configuration of (class, A. B.) forces" (Lenin, 1986b, p. 114) remained for him just "fictitious" concepts.

Before the revolution, Lenin had described at least several ideas of the future model of government. Researchers particularly quote one passage of Lenin's (Lenin, 1987b, p. 244) statement written in 1915 and describing the future system in a very clear way:

> Let us look at contemporary army. Here is one of the good examples of organization. Organization is good only when it is flexible and, at the same time, is able to dictate uniform intention to millions of people. Today these millions are sitting at their homes in various ends of the country. Mobilization order comes tomorrow, and they gather at the mobilization points. Today they are lying in trenches, sometimes over long months. Tomorrow they are attacking in a different frontline arrangement. Today they make miracles avoiding bullets and shrapnel. Tomorrow they make miracles in open battle (…). This is what we call organization, when millions of people pursuing one goal, guided by unanimous will, change the form of their co-existence and action, change the place and methods of their activities, change tools and weapons according to changing circumstance and needs of battle. This also applies to the struggle of the working class against the bourgeoisie.[5]

Let us note that when understood directly, the above is actually an *expressis verbis* definition of the principle of the militarization of labor, which was ascribed to the name of Leon Trotsky (1879–1940) during the years of war communism. This principle stated that workers were to be treated as soldiers on the labor front line. This implied subjecting workers to regulations for which military

---

[5] The underlined words were underlined by Lenin himself.

rigors were typical and involving all the consequences of this fact. For example, leaving a job was equal to desertion and was subject to military revolutionary tribunals (Данишевский, 1920, p. 21; Solzhenitsyn, 1990, p. 287). A similar principle, not expressed *expressis verbis,* was included in the first Bolshevik Labour Code adopted in the middle of 1918.

After the tsar's reign collapsed and before the Bolsheviks took power, they could implement their ideas more easily. They distinguished themselves from the other political parties in Russia AD 1917, in this case, by a specifically unusual political program. Legally published shortly after the February Revolution (but designed much earlier), it provided for the restoration of the death penalty, and "proletarian compulsion starting from shooting to death (as a) method of modeling a communist man from human material of the capitalist era" (*Программа русской социал-демократической рабочей партии,* 1917, p. 10). Apart from this, it did, however, propose a number of measures considered "progressive" by contemporary people: broad powers of local self-government, "the right for self-determination of all nations in the state", or "equal rights of women". The programme of Lenin's faction of the Russian Socialdemocratic Workers Party also included the proposal of "election of judges by the people" and "change of the professional army into levy in mass". The most important postulate was, however, about the agrarian question (*аграрный вопрос*). The RSDWP programme proposed, in this case, the "confiscation" of all private land in the country without any compensation (*Программа русской социал-демократической рабочей партии,* 1917, p. 13).

Apart from this, the Bolsheviks did not make any broader presentation of their postulates concerning the introduction of some new law before they took power. It appears that the only exception here was an article by one of the few lawyers in Lenin's party, Petr Ivanovich Stuchka (1865–1932), published by *Правда* at the end of May 1917. Stuchka proposed building two legal

systems: the common courts and, in addition to them, out-of-
-court verdicts on enemies of the revolution. The Bolshevik lawyer
also claimed that "as soon as the law ceases to conform with the
social relations, it will simply turn into a piece of paper." "You
cannot", he called on the lawmakers, "use the old laws as the basis
for the new social development just like those old laws could not
create the old social relations" (Стучка, 1917a, pp. 1–2; Стучка,
1964, pp. 225–227).[6] To reinforce his statement, Stuchka (1964)
quoted Marx who proposed to "deprive the old regime forces"
of their protection by law.[7] With this quotation in mind, Stuchka
proposed to "start at least from research (*розыск*) in the old and
new collections of laws (*уложениях*) looking for paragraphs
permitting to bring the deposed tsar and his arrested supporters
to trial" (Стучка, 1964).

While compromising with some of the existing concepts, the
Bolshevik lawyer proposes issuing a special retroactive decree
(*особый декрет с обратной силой*) against such people and
leaves no doubt as to the punishment he would choose for them.
Punishment which was not preceded by any court procedure was
an even better solution for him (Стучка, 1964).

"К. Marx also addressed this problem," Stuchka wrote. "When
a successful revolution takes place, the opponents can be hanged
but there must not be any court verdicts on them. They can be
eliminated (*убранные*)[8] like defeated enemies, but they must
not be on trial like offenders." Stuchka (1964) believed that this

---

[6]   This quotation is also discussed in Blum (Блум, 1965, pp. 190–191).

[7]   Part of this quotation read as follows: "[The laws mentioned above] grew
from old [social] relations and they should die (*погибнуть*) together with
them... This preservation of the letter of law (*почвы законности*) is intended
to preserve such private interests (*частных интересов*) as binding while in
fact they are no longer binding". The underlined words as in the original.

[8]   The Russian word *убрать* can mean „remove" as well as „murder." It seems
that the intention was to convey the second meaning to the reader, especially
during the revolution time.

solution could prevent "wasting time on looking for paragraphs and offenses at least for the miserable arrested spies and provokers". The presented reflections were the first transparent announcement that the Bolsheviks were planning a new extraordinary legal system.

Profound legal transformations were the permanent objectives of the October Revolution. These objectives had the form of four postulates: immediate withdrawal of Russia from the war, that is, declaring ceasefire, the liquidation of what they called large land property (*помещичья собственность на землю*), worker control of production, and the appointment of the Soviet Government. These postulates paved way for the complete cancellation of any property rights in the country and towns.

The *Land Decree* immediately cancelled private property of land with no compensation.[9] The document included an unprecedented statement saying that "private ownership of land is cancelled for ever" and land is to become the "property of the whole nation". Land was given out to any people demanding it but not as their property, as Soviet historiography had often suggested. Possessors had to use the land whilst having no title to it. Land could be given to all people who were willing to work on it. This was the leading criterion of allocating land. The *Land Decree* banned employing any hired labor on land and cancelled all transactions involving land (sale, lease, or disposal in any other way). This was what they called the socialization of land (since the 1930s it was referred to as nationalization in the USSR for political reasons) which the Bolsheviks had accepted from the Party of Socialist-Revolutionaries. The implementation of this conception allowed to materialize the peasants' utopia which had long existed in the minds of Russian peasants. However, at the same time all

---

[9]   Regulations of the *Decree* are quoted according to: *Собрание узаконений и распоряжений рабочего и крестьянского правительства (СУиРРиКП)*, 1917/1918. *Декреты Советской власти*, Москва 1964, Vol. 1, p. 17. The discussion of the document in the Polish language is given by, e.g. *Encyklopedia Rewolucji Październikowej*, op. cit., p. 82.

of them were stripped of their ownership title for land, something that had never happened in any country (Гойхбарг, 1921, p. 3).

From the very beginning of the Bolshevik state, the most dynamically developing branch of the law was criminal law. The Bolshevik leader identified penal regulations with repression against the enemies of the revolution. In the beginning, the Bolsheviks had intended to use the pre-revolution lawyers in the new legal system (especially justices of the peace, who were introduced under the reform of courts in 1864) (Стучка, 1917b, p. 1). This idea was, however, abandoned in connection with strong resistance from some lawyers. As a result, the Bolsheviks decided to reject the entire pre-revolutionary legal system as a one-off move. It was done by the *Decree on Courts* issued by the Council of People's Commissars on November 24, 1917, which is usually referred to by historians as the *Decree on Courts No. 1* (*Собрание узаконений и распоряжений*, 1917/1918, No. 4, item 50).

The decree abolished "all the hitherto existing general court organs (*общие судебные установления*) such as: district courts, court chambers" and "the ruling senate (the decree used lowercase letters here, A. B.) together with all its departments, military navy courts of all levels, as well as the commercial courts; all this was replaced with court organs appointed by way of democratic election".

The decree also abolished "the so far existing institutions of magistrates, prosecutor's supervision, and the institution of sworn and private attorneys".

To replace the abolished court organs, they appointed local courts (*местные суды*) consisting of one permanent judge and two additional people's lay-judges summoned to the court sittings from the list compiled by the local councils of delegates. The decree stated that the local courts were appointed through direct democratic election, and this election was to be carried out by the appointed local councils of worker, soldier, and peasant delegates.

The *Decree on Courts No. 1* ruled out the application of the whole pre-revolutionary law. The application of laws existing before the Bolshevik coup was allowed only in cases when they "were not abolished by the revolution and were not contradictory to the revolutionary conscience (*революционная совесть*) and revolutionary legal awareness (*революционное правосознание*)" (*Собрание узаконений и распоряжений*, No. 1, paragraph 5).

This was legal nihilism as understood by the new authorities, permitting to sentence anyone on principles of total discretion on the grounds of unwritten legal norms. Since the institution of appeal was also abolished (the only cassation was allowed in cases of formal deficiencies), all verdicts were final.

But it would be wrong to think that the local courts established by the *Decree on Courts No. 1* (people's courts after March 1928) performed the administration of justice in the Bolshevik state. They had the power to judge property cases up to the total worth of 3,000 roubles and to impose penalties of up to 3 years of prison (Soviet terminology: "deprivation of freedom"). All other cases were judged by the "revolutionary tribunals" established to:

> fight against the counter-revolutionary forces in order to establish barriers separating them (*miery odgrozhdeniya*) [the counter-
> -revolutionary forces, A. B.] from the revolution and its attainments, and to solve matters concerning the control of marauding (*maroderstvo*) and sabotage (*khishchnichesvo*) subversion and other fraud by merchants (*torgovtsy*) industrialists, civil servants, and other persons (*Собрание узаконений и распоряжений*, No. 1, paragraph 5).

There was no possibility to appeal against the verdicts issued by the revolutionary tribunals. The appointment of these tribunals was, in this case, the materialization of the above-mentioned proposals made by Stuchka in May 1917. This led to the emergence of legal dualism in the Bolshevik state: the system of ordinary and extraordinary courts judging political cases. After the reintroduction of the death penalty in February 1918, this penalty became the most frequent punishment used by the tribunals.

In the years of war communism, the Bolshevik state had, at different periods, a whole chain of revolutionary tribunals. There existed ordinary revolutionary tribunals, military revolutionary tribunals, the revolutionary tribunals of print, and the railway revolutionary tribunals famous for being very cruel in their verdicts on perpetrators of railway and transport subversion. Punishments employed by the revolutionary tribunals were not precisely defined in any of the normative acts. There were only norms of a technical character; instructions describing the sequence of phases in the procedures for the juries did not have *ex lege* education in law.

Unwritten law was strongly promoted in Bolshevik Russia during the entirety of the war communism period. For example, the implementation of the people's law (*народное право*) was supported, the law which "should be expressed directly by the judges in which these judges should not be restricted by the bonds of written law" (Смирнов, Портнов, Славин, 1990, p. 36). They also officially rejected the principle of the independence of courts. Stuchka wrote about this rule in the middle of 1918: "the right to elect judges should belong to the councils as organs holding all power and the sole exponent of the outlooks and desirers of the worker--peasant democracy" (Стучка, 1918, p. 5).

The councils of delegates were the organs authorized to determine the date of the election and tenure of the judges:

> The elected courts, the author went on, can be recalled (*otozvany*) at any time by the given council. In this way the People's Judge is deprived of the previously alleged "independence" and "irremovability" of the bourgeois judge but he obtained a durable (*prochnaya*) autonomy which earns him people's trust (*narodnoe doverie*). No one can exert pressure on his conscience by threatening to transfer him or apply disciplinary responsibility. The people's judge depends only on the people's trust he enjoys. Plans and prospects (to build personal career, benefits) are not the motivation to become a judge. The motivation is

only the social duty and social mission (*obshchestvennoe prizvanie*) (Стучка, 1918, p. 5).

The Bolshevik state used a similar method to justify the absence of any law-abidingness guarantees (the very term law-abidingness was rejected at the beginning). The described concepts, although original in some respects, were employed to justify the purely political nature of reprisal. However, the revolutionary tribunals turned out to be not very efficient in use.

The peak of repression came with the All-Russian Extraordinary Committee for the Fight Against Counterrevolution and Sabotage (Cheka) headed from its inception by F. Dzerzhinski (1877–1926). The Cheka was not established by any normative act. Hence, even the official name of this institution never existed. Sometimes it was named the Extraordinary Committee for the Fight against Counterrevolution, Sabotage, and Profiteering, sometimes this name was expanded by adding "...and Service Offenses". The Cheka powers comprised preparatory proceedings, sending people to prison and concentration camps, issuing verdicts and executions.

The first chronicler of the described institution, deputy head of the Cheka Martin Ivanovich Lacis (1888–1938), provides the following account of the committee's powers in a low circulation book published in Moscow in 1920:

> Cheka is not an investigation committee or a court. It is not a tribunal either. It is a combat organ operating on the internal front of the civil war, using in its battles the powers (*приемы*) of investigation committees, courts, tribunals, and army troops (*военные силы*). It does not try the enemy but destroys it. It does not pardon the enemy but turns into ashes (*испепеляет*) anyone who holds weapons on the other side of the barricade and who cannot be used (*использован*) by us in any way (Лацис, 1921, p. 8).[10]

---

[10]   Some excerpts from Lacis's statements are quoted by, among other authors, R. Pipes (Pipes, 1994, p. 655), but in an imperfect translation.

Further parts of the book tell us about the penal measures applied by the committee. According to Dzerzhynsky's deputy, the Cheka "terminates without court proceedings on the offence site or isolates from society by sending to concentration camps (*концентрационный лагерь*), sends [the case] to the tribunal whenever the case requires a similar solution and broad publicity" (Лацис, 1921, p. 8).

Reprisal was very widely used until the end of the war communism era. Sometimes this was done also on the grounds of the adopted normative regulations. Among the best-known of these were the *Decree of the Council of People's Commissaries, The socialist fatherland in distress* (February 21, 1918), and the *Decree on Red Terror* dated September 5, 1918, which promoted overt and arbitrary terror. The most famous document, the *Decree on Red Terror*, said for instance, that "under the existing situation, protection of the hinterland with the use of terror is an absolute necessity". The Decree therefore provided for

> sending a large number of responsible party comrades to the hinterland, the necessity to protect the Soviet Republic against class enemies by isolating them in concentration camps, shooting all persons who had been in contact (*prikosnovennye*) with White Guard organizations, conspiracy, and rebels (*Собрание узаконений и распоряжений*, 1917/1918, No. 65, item 710).[11]

No comprehensive list of penal measures was compiled in Bolshevik Russia until the end of war communism. Criminal law also adopted the principle of analogy, thus rejecting the principle of *nullum crimen, nulla poena sine lege*. But a normative act was issued

---

[11] Reprinted in: *Еженедельник Чрезвычайных Комиссий по борьбе с контрреволюцией и спекуляцией*, 1918, No. 1, p. 11 (where the resolution is signed only by the secretary of the Council of the People's Commissaries and Lenin's personal secretary L. Fotieva) and the *Декреты Советской власти*, 1964, pp. 291–292.

to mention examples of penal measures. Such an act, described as the *Guiding Principles of Russian Penal Legislation*, and published in December 1919, listed the following penal measures:

a) reproach (*внушение*), b) public reproach, c) compelling to action which was not a physical offence (e.g. attending an education course), d) announcing a boycott [of a given person] (*объявление под бойкотом*), e) relegation from a union (*объединения*) for a specific time (*на время*) or forever, f) return or, whenever this was impossible, reparation of the wrongs, g) deposition, h) ban from performing a specific activity or other activities or a specific job or other jobs, i) confiscation of all or part of the property, j) stripping of political rights, k) declaration of being an enemy of the revolution or the people (*объявление врагом революции или народа*), l) forced labour (*принудительные работы*) without transfer to limited freedom establishments, m) imprisonment for a specified or unspecified period (*неопределенный срок*) until a given event (*известное событие*) takes place, n) outlawry (*объявление вне закона*), o) *execution by shooting*, p) *combination of the above-mentioned penal measures* (*Руководящие начала по уголовному праву РСФСР, 1919*, ch. VI, paragraph 25).

Bolshevik lawyers kept trying to establish a new science of law until the end of the civil war in Russia. The leading role in research work after the middle of 1918 was played by the Socialist Academy of Social Sciences (among the members were A. Goikhbarg, M. Reisner, P. Stuchka and others). New branches of law were also developed, such as labor law (*трудовое законодательство*) or agrarian law (*земельное право*). But also in these cases the law was subordinated to political tasks. This applied also to civil law which the authorities had planned to eliminate after some time. So a number of legal acts were issued to limit the institution of property rights and later remove them entirely.

As regards rural property, this goal was achieved by the *Decree of the Council of People's Commissaries on the Socialization of Land* adopted in February 1918 (*Собрание узаконений* и *распоряжений*, 1917/1918, No. 25, item 346). The right to rural property was removed by the *Decree on Cancelling Private Property in Towns* (*Собрание узаконений и распоряжений*, 1918, No. 62, item 674), designed entirely by Lenin. In June 1918, hereditary rights were also abrogated (except for household goods).

As mentioned above, the lawyers close to the new power center tried to promote the ideas of the new science of law during the years of war communism. They sometimes promoted the ideas of social solidarity, the extinction of law, and the need to abandon the written law in a communist society. The most outstanding specialist in civil law of that time, Goikhbarg (1918, pp. 9–10, cited in Гойхбарг, 1919, p. 37), contended that under the communist system

> the period of social struggle and war will become just a legend (...) Compulsion as a category of inter-human relations will cease to exist. So will law as an instrument of compulsion in social relations, as the expression of continuous struggle between individuals, groups, and the state. With a deep consolidation [of the principles] of collectivism, not only civil law but law as a whole will cease to exist. The harmonious existence of people will not be built on the foundation of social compulsion and social need, in other words, on the foundation of law, but on the grounds of total social freedom.[12]

A similar theory which Goikhbarg linked with the name of Leon Duguit was described in the USSR as the theory of the law's social functions. The reality of Bolshevik Russia was, however, totally different than that described by Goikhbarg, who was, to some extent, also involved in the terror of the period.

During war communism, the Bolsheviks established a complete and consistent, though unprecedented system of a totalitarian state in Russia. This system was characterized by:

---

[12] The quoted excerpt is from Goikhbarg's text, also found in Goldman (1983, p. 185).

1. The practical application of Lenin's pre-revolutionary comprehension of law where law was an instrument of reprisal against enemies of the authorities unable to restrict the lawmaker (a combination of Marxism and legal nihilism).
2. The rejection *de iure* of all legal guarantees protecting the rights of the citizens; the rejection of the entire pre-revolutionary legislation and replacing it with never defined, random regulations of the unwritten law.
3. The introduction of legal dualism: the common courts and the extraordinary courts which judged political cases; establishing a wide range of reprisal institutions (four types of revolutionary tribunals) in this administrative repression (the Cheka).
4. The liquidation of property law (real estate) in towns and in the country, on the whole territory of the state.
5. The concentration of all power in the hands of executive organs; replacing the institution of parliamentary act (with the parliament itself preserved in place) by a normative act of the executive authorities (extremely broad conception of the decree); the official negation of the institution of separation of powers.

To sum up, it may be said that during the three and a half years of war communism Russia experienced vast transformations. At the same time, a totally new, unprecedented legal and political system was established. Most probably none (maybe except for the transformations in Cambodia under Pol Pot) of the other totalitarian systems of the 20th century brought about such deep changes into a pre-revolutionary state. Thus, it is no coincidence that many of the concepts related to the Bolshevik state were adopted during the Stalin era. Some of the institutions, in a limited form, also infiltrated into the Nazi legal system (the nihilism of R. Freisler, the dualism of the administration of justice, maybe even the institution of the family code and related upbringing concepts). But many more of the Bolshevik ideas of law and politics originating in the war communism period entered the legal systems of the USSR and the communist bloc countries. Some of the institutions which were developed under the Bolshevik state continue to exist even in the Polish legal system in the present day. This applies, among other regulations, to the well-known general clauses in the Polish Civil Code such as the principle of social life and the socio-economic role of the law.

Key words: The Russian revolution, totalitarianism, war communism, genocide, political repressions, bolshevism, Lenin, law under totalitarian regime, political system of totalitarianism, civil law in totalitarianism, utopianism.

Kształtowanie się pierwszego państwa totalitarnego: system polityczny i prawny Rewolucji Rosyjskiej (październik 1917–1921) i jego konsekwencje

Artykuł analizuje kształtowanie się bolszewickiego systemu politycznego i prawnego, powstałego w latach komunizmu wojennego 1917–1921 i wcześniej: w programie partii i jej założyciela. Poglądy Lenina, który na temat prawa pisał bardzo niewiele, a w Rosji carskiej traktowany był jako postać marginalna, stanowiły niewątpliwy asumpt do wytworzenia systemu totalitarnego. Natomiast program partii, jeszcze w początku 1917 roku deklarujący literalnie wolności obywatelskie czy przywiązanie do demokracji bezpośredniej, został po rewolucji całkowicie złamany. Lata komunizmu wojennego to bowiem stworzenie bardzo rozbudowanego systemu ludobójstwa oraz bardzo szerokich kompetencyjnie organów represyjnych, ograniczenia praw obywatelskich i najbardziej podstawowych swobód (z prawem własności włącznie), przy deklarowaniu bardzo szerokich wolności, nieobecnych w żadnym innym systemie politycznym. Nietrudno dostrzec, że negatywne dziedzictwo takiego systemu odbiło się na systemach polityczno-prawnych wielu państw, w tym Polski. Bolszewicka rewolucja 1917 roku jest w tym przypadku najgorszym chyba wydarzeniem XX stulecia.

Формирование первого тоталитарного государства: политическая и правовая система Русской революции (октябрь 1917–1921 гг.) и ее последствия

В статье рассматривается формирование большевистской политической и правовой системы, созданной в годы военного коммунизма 1917–1921 гг., и ранее: в программе партии и ее основателя. Ленин, взгляды которого были решающими в формировании тоталитарной системы, в царской России по вопросам права писал мало и был скорее фигурой маргинальной. Программа партии, еще вначале 1917 года декларирующая гражданские свободы и ценность прямой демократии, после революции была полностью изменена. Годы военного коммунизма – это создание системы геноцида и репрессивных органов с широкими полномочиями, ограничение гражданских прав и основных свобод (включая право собственности) при декларировании очень широких свобод, отсутствующих в любой другой политической системе. Несложно увидеть, что негативное наследие такой системы повлияло на политико-правовые системы многих стран, включая Польшу. Большевистская революция 1917 года, с этой точки зрения, является худшим событием 20-го века.

DOI: 10.12797/9788376389042.03

Lyudmila Ilyicheva ⓘD https://orcid.org/0000-0002-0223-6418
The Russian Presidential Academy of National Economy and Public
Administration

Chapter 2

State, Business and Society in Russia: The Genesis and Models of Interaction 1917–2017

After more than a century since the Russian Revolution a relatively sufficient amount of time has passed to pay attention to the lessons of the revolution and now really clarify what in fact what has happened in the intervening years.

Before 1914 the class of entrepreneurs already looked quite formed, and the period from 1908 to 1914 can rightfully be called the golden age of capitalism in Russia. The capital of newly established joint-stock companies during that period comprised 41% of the total capital of all business societies organized after 1861. Between 1908 and 1914 more than 70% of new investments were created by domestic funds.

This wealth, distributed in a very uneven manner, was evidenced by the twofold increase of deposits in banks savings and current bank accounts as well as the fact that Russian citizens began to actively buy back securities that had long been in the hands of foreigners. Hence there were positive tendencies in the relationships between the state and entrepreneurs in accordance with the course taken by Witte and continued by Stolypin. The period from 1905 to 1914 may be deemed the time of emergence of a class of real entrepreneurs and a market for private demand able to replace state encouragement in all economic sectors both in the city and in the countryside.

By the beginning of World War I, an extensive network of representative bodies of capital had achieved great influence within society. Any potential attempts to extend influence over the state authorities in the first post-reform years were replaced by a powerful organizational pressure on the government resulting in the entwinement of public and private interests. The significant economic success achieved by capitalist Russia was definitely a result of the unwritten contract between the state and the capital although the latter's aspirations did not always coincide with the political and economic interests of the state.

In 1915–1916, during the military and economic crisis, various social structures were established in the country. Their purpose was to help the state to find a way out in the situation of economic collapse. Upon the initiative of the business leader A. Guchkov, the head of the Octobrist Party, a Central Military Industrial Committee was set up. This committee distributed military contracts among business leaders having sufficient authority in politics and acted practically as a parallel government.

In 1917 "The Society for the Economic Revival of Russia" was one of the most affluent political groups. It was founded thanks to the initiative of A. Putilin. It included bankers and industrialists from Petrograd (Saint Petersburg). The organization had 269 branches. In Moscow, during this period, the opulent organized the "All-Russian Union of Trade and Industry" which included about 500 different business associations. One of the tasks of the Union was the preparation for leading its placemen to the Fifth State Duma and after the February Revolution – to the Constituent Convention. These facts illustrate the formation of diversified ties between the economy and politics, their interdependence and interconnection.

The alliance of industrialists and authorities, broken by the revolutionary events, was partially restored during the period of New Economic Policy (hereinafter referred to as "NEP"). A new stage in the interaction between political structures and new entrepreneurs began. This temporary deviation from the extremely rigid Soviet statist policy and control once again demonstrated the great importance of such ties. At the same time researchers note contradictions, such as obvious inconsistency on part of the authorities in the implementation of this approach.

At the end of 1921 the Leninist formula of "state capitalism" is enriched with the concept of "transfer of state enterprises to so-called economic accounting", i.e. "largely on commercial, capitalist grounds". This provision is critical not only for the NEP period but also for the comprehension of the entrepreneurship phenomenon with regard to state-owned enterprises. The transfer of such enterprises, especially trusts, to full economic accounting, i.e. to full economic responsibility for the manufacture, nomenclature and sales of products, allows for a discussion on state entrepreneurship.

It is important to emphasize that during the formation of state self-supporting trusts there were many examples of merging the interests of trusts' management and business speculators who made great profit from trade and intermediary services with these trusts rather than organizing production and trade themselves in their civilized capitalist forms. By 1924 private capital controlled over two-thirds of the wholesale and retail goods turnover in the country aggravating strong mismanagement of the new bodies, whose leadership came from the liquidated central administrations and centers, taught how to deal with the distribution of goods but lacking genuine knowledge about the organization of trade and market. It can be said without exaggeration that elements of parasitic, speculative-bureaucratic capitalism were born. They did not have anything to do with the patterns of capitalism that existed in developed European capitalist countries.

In the Soviet Union, since it was a totalitarian system, "corporatism" was characterized by a relatively close integrated connection of various corporate interests with the "nationwide interest".

There were corporate interests, sometimes realized contrary to the interests of other corporate groups, in the economic monopoly system regulated by the state. For example, investments in agriculture were carried out through the development of food and consumer goods industries which ultimately affected the development of agriculture. This predominantly refers to the development of the military-industrial complex.

The time of "Perestroyka" resulted in different phenomena: existing interest groups actually undermined the party bodies and, remaining uncontrolled, began to manage resources entering the power struggle with each other. The abolishment of central planning (the CPSU) freed the groups of interests from the support of party bodies. The particular groups became the main power brokers in the post-Soviet area, and still do not have either serious political opposition or serious economic competitors. At the same time, however, these groups were being transformed. The interest in the "participation in redistribution of resources" implies the unification or delimitation of the subjects of this redistribution on contractual terms. This initiated the formation of "elite groups" which strengthened the power structures.

At the end of the 1990s the actually authoritarian and oligarchic power mechanisms came into conflict with the society's need for broad social reforms. A balanced system of constructively functioning political parties and other socio-political organizations was not created in society. The low level of trust of the population towards power was fixed. This determined the nature and specific features of lobbyism within public authorities, strengthening their diversification, mobility and adaptability. Naturally, they desired to overcome the negative attitude of the overwhelming and silent majority toward the political decision-makers.

New interests called for new mechanisms for their implementation. They focused not only on economic but also on political processes. There was a fusion of interests of the upper class of the financial and economic elite and interests of the upper bureaucracy as well as crystallization and confrontation of various oligarchic financial and industrial groups in interaction with various groups of state bureaucracy. Corporations tried to lobby their interests through such political forms as social associations. Such channels of influence as latent and sometimes open investment of capital in politics, especially in the electoral process, were legalized.

In practice the criminalization of Russian society was intensified. Hidden lobbyism and corruption in the top echelons of power are among the top ten most important Russian problems. This required the adoption and implementation of the program of struggle against organized crime and corruption. The task of regulatory measures towards the state apparatus of colleges, ministries and social councils under the government and parliament came into force.

When Vladimir Putin took the office of the President of the Russian Federation the country entered the process of cardinal reconstruction. First of all, the relationships between power and society, political institutions, social groups and nations, between the state and social associations and political parties, between the center and regions, the relationships within the federal subjects, between business and society, business and political parties etc. radically changed. Political relations began to be formed in a more democratic manner.

Paradoxically, nowadays there is a greater diversity of regional interests and social forms of life. Regional authorities assume the functions of developers and conductors of economic and social policy thereby developing and strengthening the specificity of their regions.

With the advent of the world economic crisis in 2008, Russia set upon the path of modernization with the goal of reaching a national consensus in relation to the long-term goals of economic development. Such long-term strategic goals become a mobilizing program of actions when methods and mechanisms of their achievement are developed, resources necessary for their achievement are identified, including support of the goals by the crucial social groups and, ideally, by the whole of society. This task was accepted for implementation (comp. Mau, 2015).

Map of modernization project in the Russian Federation

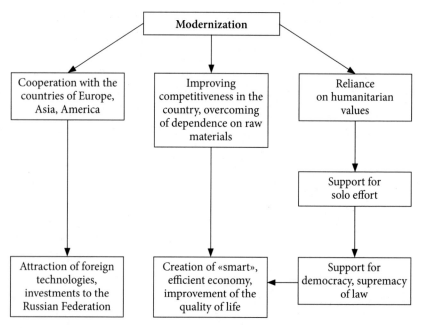

Contrary to the destructive doctrines of the past, the current leadership of the country has set the task of maintaining relations with other countries as equal partners in order to mutually enrich their cultures and economies, to solve security problems etc.

In his decrees from May 2012, Vladimir Putin instructed the government to take measures aimed at the improvement of Russia's position in the World Bank's rating for business climate from the 120th position, calculated in 2011, to the 50th in 2015 and to the 20th in 2018.

If one refers to the annual "Conduct of Business" report by the World Bank, it will be brought to light that this report has already been compiled for the 14th time and covers 190 countries. The report focuses on the regulatory standards that facilitate or hinder business development throughout the entire business cycle including the establishment of enterprises, conduct of business, carrying out foreign trade activity, payment of taxes as well as maintaining a high level of protection of the rights of investors.

The WB analysts in the latest reports looked at three main scenarios for the development of the Russian economy. In the baseline scenario, the World Bank expects that the average oil price will stay at $53.2 per barrel in 2015 and $56.9 per barrel in 2017. As noted in the report, if the impact of sanctions and the decline in oil prices continues, it will provoke a prolonged recession in Russia. "Based on the continuing geopolitical tensions, the present forecast assumes preservation of the sanctions during 2015 and 2017." The cost of attracting foreign borrowing remains high, and access to international capital markets – limited, which will hold the investment demand (World Bank, 2015, comp. also World Bank, 2017).

The problems mentioned above are not fulfilling the modernization agenda in the current crisis. Other important areas of institutional and structural reforms should be highlighted, such as industries of human capital (education, healthcare and the pension system), which are now closely intertwining social, fiscal and investment factors. New approaches to social policy, foreign economic activity and spatial development are required.

In conclusion, the urgent tasks that require creative institutional solutions for the further transformation of the economic system of Russia (as a post-communist state), can be described in a number of points:

- updating the most important components of market infra-structure (banking systems, stock market, infrastructure, support for small and medium-sized businesses, and others);
- taking decisive steps against the sprawling corruption and other forms of negative shadow relations in the economy;
- taking effective measures to implement major structural changes in the economy, associated with the departure from the raw material model and the conversion to the innovation-oriented model of economic development;
- creating an effective national innovation system;
- re-creating a long-term forecasting system, strategic and indicative planning and programming of social and economic development at the federal level;
- discovering effective forms of the project-based approach to solving repetitively emerging large-scale scientific, technological and socio-economic problems across the whole country;
- the creation of a more effective mechanism of interaction between enterprise structures and the state in the implementation of relevant national issues;
- significant improvement of the system of regional management of the economy, which should contribute to the expansion of centralized influence towards more balanced territorial development and stimulation of initiative efforts of the regions in addressing socio-economic problems at the regional and local level (comp. Орлова, Соколова, 2017).

Current objectives determine the perspectives of development of the Russian economy and the priorities of the state with regard to the economic policy. The success of their implementation is directly connected with the characteristics of the institutional structure of the country and its civilizational peculiarities, the values and interests of the major economic actors that are forming a real mechanism of public policy.

It also seems possible to name a set of useful principles underlying the relationship between the state, business and society in Russia:

- determined refusal to merge the functions of private entrepreneurship and public administration;
- transparency of relations between large capital and state power, based on law and the institutions available for control by civil society;
- effective participation in the system of social partnership on the basis of collective agreements, the exclusion of force methods in solving disputable problems (comp. Dudin, 2014).

To sum up, the solution for overcoming the dark legacy of the Revolution, which lies not only in ineffectiveness but also in the split between the three constructing pillars of the nation, is to work out a new model of harmonious interaction between the state, business and society in Russia. The oversimplified (and in this way deconstructed) idea of cooperation between the three elements needs to undergo gradual and consistent rebirth in the seemingly trivial process of implementing public-private partnerships.

Państwo, biznes i społeczeństwo w Rosji: powstanie i modele interakcji 1917–2017

Rozdział przedstawia genezę interakcji pomiędzy biznesem, państwem i społeczeństwem po rewolucji 1917 roku. Zaznaczono rolę przedsiębiorczości na wszystkich etapach rozwoju socjalistycznego oraz postsocjalistycznego. Obecne stadium charakteryzuje się poszukiwaniem równowagi interesów pomiędzy państwem, biznesem a społeczeństwem oraz próbą jej utrzymania. Sferę innowacji można określić jako proces implementacji partnerstwa publiczno--prywatnego.

Государство, бизнес и общество в России: генезис и модели взаимодействия 1917–2017 гг.

Глава представляет генезис взаимодействия бизнеса, государства и общества после революции 1917 года. Отмечена роль предпринимательства на всех этапах социалистического и постсоциалистического развития. Нынешний этап характеризуется поиском и попыткой сохранения баланса интересов между государством, бизнесом и обществом. Сфера инноваций может быть определена как процесс имплементации государственно-частного партнерства.

DOI: 10.12797/9788376389042.04

IVAN FOMIN ⓘD https://orcid.org/0000-0003-4703-5262
Immanuel Kant Baltic Federal University, Kaliningrad

Chapter 3

Contested Post-Soviet Secessions in the Russian Political Discourse: The Grammar of Recognition[1]

This chapter is focused on the cases of recognition of contested secessionist entities in the official Russian political discourse. Of all the post-Soviet contested states there are only three that have been officially recognized by Russia. They are Abkhazia, South Ossetia and Crimea. In other cases, even though Russia did sometimes back the secessionist entities, it has never formally recognized their independence. For example, Novorossiya (the Donetsk Peoples' Republic and the Lugansk Peoples' Republic) in Ukraine and Transnistria in Moldova did receive Russia's support and petitioned to be recognized by Moscow (and even to be integrated as regions of Russia), but are still deprived of recognition.

---

[1] This work was supported by the National Science Centre in Poland (grant No. 2015/19/B/HS5/02516).

The goal of my research is to understand how Russia's official political discourses about the entities that did receive Moscow's recognition (Abkhazia, South Ossetia and Crimea) differ from each other in terms of discursive strategies used to legitimize their statuses. This analysis is a way to better understand how the painful legacies of the Soviet era and the revolutionary momentum of the de-composition of the Soviet empire in 1991 echo in the contemporary political language of Russia. The study also outlines a spectrum of how the political discourse of Russia reacts to the still ongoing processes of disintegration in the post-Soviet space.

Comparing the cases of Abkhazia, South Ossetia and Crimea can be productive, since, on the one hand, they share a number of common features with both Georgia and Ukraine being post--Soviet polities, both dealing with the conflictogenic legacy of the Soviet territorial policies, both going through color revolutions in mid-2000s and both facing Russia's interventions. However, when it comes to the secessionist entities themselves, they are quite different in terms of the history of these territories and their ethnolinguistic demography.

Russia's policies towards these entities are also not identical. Abkhazia and South Ossetia have been recognized as separate states, but have not been fully integrated into Russia (even though South Ossetia has petitioned several times for this to happen), while Crimea was made a part of Russia almost immediately after the de-facto separation from Ukraine.

Materials and Methods

The research is based on the comparative analysis of two texts:
1) the statement by Dmitry Medvedev on the recognition of Abkhazia and South Ossetia (August 26, 2008),

2) the address by Vladimir Putin on the reunification of Crimea with Russian Federation ("the Crimean Speech") (March 18, 2014).

The main analytical category that I use in this research is that of *topos*. *Topoi* can be described as argumentation strategies that belong to either explicit or inferable premises. "They are the content-related warrants or 'conclusion rules' that connect the argument or arguments with the conclusion, the claim. As such, they justify the transition from the argument or arguments to the conclusion" (Reisigl and Wodak, 2001, pp. 74–75). The abductive approach to topoi analysis that is often used in the Discourse-Historic Approach to critical discourse analysis has a number of limitations when it comes to its universal use, however it can be quite effective in describing and comparing the argumentation strategies that are typical for certain discourses and genres.

The list of topoi that I analyzed from the studied declarations is presented in Table 1 (based on Reisigl and Wodak, 2001, pp. 74––80). In order to compare the two documents, I used quantitative analysis counting the number of paragraphs in which each of the topoi was used.

Table 1.
List of Topoi

Topoi	Conclusion rule
Topos of danger	If there are specific dangers and threats, one should do something about them.
Topos of democracy	If a decision does (not) conform to democratic procedures, one should (not) accept it.
Topos of diversity	If a political action or decision does (not) respect the diversity of society, one should (not) perform or make it.
Topos of ethnicity	If a political action or decision does (not) respect the interests of an ethnic group, one should (not) perform or make it.

Topos of history	One should perform (omit) a specific action, because of historical analogies, negative and positive examples or other similarities ("history teaches that…").
Topos of humanitarianism	If a political action or decision does (not) conform to human rights or humanitarian convictions and values, one should (not) perform or make it.
Topos of intuition	If a claim conforms to one's intuition (feeling), the claim is true.
Topos of language	If a political action or decision does (not) respect the interests of a language community, one should (not) perform or make it.
Topos of law	If a law or an otherwise codified norm prescribes (forbids) a specific action, the action has to be performed (omitted).
Topos of numbers	If the numbers prove a specific claim, this claim is true.
Topos of peace	If a political action or decision does (not) conform to the value of peace, one should (not) perform or make it.
Topos of public (*Argumentum ad populum*)	A proposition is true, good or right because many people believe it to be so.
Topos of reality	Since reality is as it is, a specific action/decision should be performed/made.
Topos of reason	If a political action or decision does (not) conform to common sense, one should (not) perform or make it.
Topos of rightness	If a situation does (not) conform to one's concept of justice (fairness, rightness, responsibility), the situation should not (should) be changed.

Results

The results of the comparative quantitative topoi analysis of the two texts are presented in Table 2 and Diagram 1.

Table 2.

Comparative Analysis of Topoi Use in the Crimean Speech (2014) and in the Statement on the Recognition of Abkhazia and South Ossetia (2008) (N of paragraphs)

Topoi	Statement on the recognition of Abkhazia and South Ossetia	Crimean Speech
Topos of danger	7	19
Topos of democracy	3	10
Topos of diversity	0	2
Topos of ethnicity	3	17
Topos of history	1	21
Topos of humanitarianism	3	6
Topos of intuition	0	2
Topos of language	0	7
Topos of law	2	14
Topos of numbers	1	7
Topos of peace	3	5
Argumentum ad populum	3	9
Topos of reality	1	1
Topos of reason	1	0
Topos of rightness	0	6
Total number of paragraphs	**11**	**64**

Diagram 1.

Comparative Analysis of Topoi Use in the Crimean Speech (2014) and in the Statement on the Recognition of Abkhazia and South Ossetia (2008) (% of paragraphs)

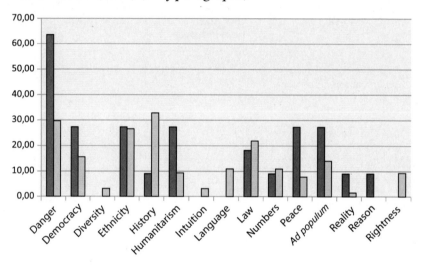

■ Abkhazia and South Ossetia ▨ Crimea

From this analysis we can see that, in general, the sets of topoi used in the two texts are quite similar. However, there are four topoi that are unique for the discourse of the Crimean Speech and one topos that is specific for the statement about South Ossetia and Abkhazia.

Diversity and Ethnicity

The first topos that is unique for the discourse about Crimea is the *topos of diversity*. It is used in the part of the text that is devoted to the ethnolinguistic demography of Crimea and to the claim that Crimea should be trilingual:

(1) Crimea is a **unique blend of different peoples' cultures and traditions.** This makes it similar to Russia as a whole, where not a single ethnic group has been lost over the centuries. Russians and Ukrainians, Crimean Tatars and people of other ethnic groups have lived side by side in Crimea, retaining their own identity, traditions, languages and faith.

(2) We have **great respect for people of all the ethnic groups** living in Crimea. This is their common home, their motherland, and it would be right – I know the local population supports this – for Crimea to have three equal national languages: Russian, Ukrainian and Tatar.

The absence of the topos of diversity in the text about South Ossetia and Abkhazia is quite illustrative since the Georgian population of the secessionist republics is radically excluded from Medvedev's discourse. Even though the topos of ethnicity is shared by both analyzed texts, neither Georgian refugees (IDP) nor those Georgians who still live in Abkhazia and South Ossetia were mentioned in Medvedev's speech. The only ethnic groups mentioned in the text are Abkhazians and Ossetians[2]. In contrast, in the Crimean Speech, Putin refers not only to Russians, but to Crimean Tatars and Ukrainians as well.

This can be explained by the context of the recognition of South Ossetia and Abkhazia since during the war of 2008 in South Ossetia Georgian villages were destroyed and the Georgian population was forced to leave. The president of South Ossetia Eduard Kokoity then declared: "We do not intend to let anybody in here anymore" (Габуев, 2008).

---

[2]   See examples in (13), (22), (23), (24).

Language

In the Crimean Speech, the topos of diversity is closely connected with another unique argumentation strategy that is the *topos of language*. In the declaration of 2014, Putin emphasized that the annexation of Crimea was connected with the threat to Russian-speaking population and was triggered by the disrespect of its language rights:

(3) Time and time again **attempts were made to deprive Russians of their historical memory, even of their language** and to subject them to forced assimilation.

(4) The new so-called authorities began by introducing **a draft law to revise the language policy**, which was a direct infringement on the rights of ethnic minorities.

(5) Those who opposed the coup were immediately threatened with repression. Naturally, the first in line here was Crimea, **the Russian-speaking Crimea.**

Rightness and Intuition

Another topos that is present in the Crimean Speech but is not used in the statement on the recognition of Abkhazia and South Ossetia is the *topos of intuition*. When speaking about the annexation of Crimea, Putin twice refers to the idea that "in people's heart" Crimea "has always been a part of Russia".

The topos of intuition is closely connected with the *topos of rightness* that is also used only in Putin's text. It is crucial to emphasize that the concept of *rightness* used by Putin does not necessarily imply equity or legal justice. It rather refers to the intuitive feeling of *spravedlivost'* (*rightness).*

Here are some fragments from the speech in which Putin refers to intuition and rightness:

(6) **In people's hearts and minds,** Crimea has always been an inseparable part of Russia. This firm conviction is based on **truth and justice** and was passed from generation to generation, over time, under any circumstances, despite all the dramatic changes our country went through during the entire 20th century.

(7) However, the people could not reconcile themselves to this **outrageous historical injustice.** All these years, citizens and many public figures came back to this issue, saying that Crimea is historically Russian land and Sevastopol is a Russian city. Yes, we all knew this **in our hearts and minds,** but we had to proceed from the existing reality and build our good-neighbourly relations with independent Ukraine on a new basis.

Another aspect of the *topos of rightness* is based on the concept of moral responsibility. It is used both to justify Russia's actions and to condemn the actions of the "western partners":

(8) Naturally, we could not leave this plea unheeded; we could not abandon Crimea and its residents in distress. This would have been **betrayal** on our part.

(9) And with Ukraine, our western partners have crossed the line, playing the bear and acting **irresponsibly and unprofessionally.**

Interestingly, the intuitive topoi of the Crimean Speech contrast with the *topos of reason* that can be found only in the Medvedev's declaration about Abkhazia and South Ossetia. This topos is used in the speech as a way to disprove Georgia's aggression against South Ossetia:

(10) The Georgian leadership, in violation of the UN Charter and their obligations under international agreements and **contrary to the voice of reason,** unleashed an armed conflict victimizing innocent civilians.

Danger

As to the topoi that were not unique for one of the analyzed discourses but were dominant in one of them, in the case of Medvedev's speech that was the *topos of danger*. In more than 60% of the paragraphs of the statement, Medvedev refers to Tbilisi threatening the very existence of the Ossetian and Abkhazian peoples. And it is this danger that was used as the main warrant to justify the recognition of the secessionist states.

For example:

(11) The Georgian leadership, in violation of the UN Charter and their obligations under international agreements and contrary to the voice of reason, **unleashed an armed conflict victimizing innocent civilians. The same fate lay in store for Abkhazia.** Obviously, they in Tbilisi hoped for a blitz-krieg that would have confronted the world community with an accomplished fact. The most inhuman way was chosen to achieve the objective – **annexing South Ossetia through the annihilation of a whole people**.

In some cases the topos of danger was combined with the *topoi of peace and humanitarianism*:

(12) It stands quite clear now: **a peaceful resolution of the conflict was not part of Tbilisi's plan**. The Georgian leadership was methodically **preparing for war**, while the political and material support provided by their foreign guardians only served to reinforce the perception of their own impunity.

(13) Tbilisi made its choice during the night of August 8, 2008. Saakashvili opted for **genocide** to accomplish his political objectives. By doing so he himself dashed all the hopes for the **peaceful coexistence** of Ossetians, Abkhazians and Georgians in a single state.

(14) Russia calls on other states to follow its example. This is not an easy choice to make, but it represents **the only possibility to save human lives**.

In the Crimean Speech, the *topos of danger* was also one of the dominant ones. For example, Putin used the threat of NATO as one of the warrants to justify the integration of Crimea.

(15) Let me note too that we have already heard declarations from Kiev about Ukraine soon joining NATO. What would this have meant for Crimea and Sevastopol in the future? It would have meant that NATO's navy would be right there in this city of Russia's military glory, and this would create not an illusory but **a perfectly real threat to the whole of southern Russia**. These are things that could have become reality were it not for the choice the Crimean people made, and I want to say thank you to them for this.

Putin also used the topos of danger arguing that there was a threat to the Russian-speaking population of Crimea after "Nationalists, neo-Nazis, Russophobes and anti-Semites" executed the coup in Ukraine:

(16) Those who opposed the coup were immediately **threatened with repression**. Naturally, the first in line here was Crimea, the Russian-speaking Crimea. In view of this, the residents of Crimea and Sevastopol turned to Russia for help in **defending their rights and lives, in preventing the events that were unfolding and are still underway in Kiev, Donetsk, Kharkov and other Ukrainian cities.**

Naturally, we could not leave this plea unheeded; we could not abandon Crimea and its residents **in distress**. This would have been betrayal on our part.

History

Even though the *topos of danger* was crucial for the discourse of the Crimean Speech, it was not the main topos used in it. The dominant topos of the speech was the *topos of history*. In more than 30% of the paragraphs, Putin appealed to it claiming that

Crimea should be a part of Russia because of the deep historical connection between them and because Crimea had been separated from Russia as a result of an "outrageous historical injustice":

(17) More than 82 percent of the electorate took part in the vote. Over 96 percent of them spoke out in favour of reuniting with Russia. These numbers speak for themselves.
      To understand the reason behind such a choice it is enough to know the **history of Crimea and what Russia and Crimea have always meant for each other**.

(18) However, the people could not reconcile themselves to this **outrageous historical injustice.** All these years, citizens and many public figures came back to this issue, saying that Crimea is **historically Russian land** and Sevastopol is a Russian city. Yes, we all knew this in our hearts and minds, but we had to proceed from the existing reality and build our good-neighbourly relations with independent Ukraine on a new basis.

(19) For all the internal processes within the organisation, NATO remains a military alliance, and we are against having a military alliance making itself at home right in our backyard or in **our historic territory.**

Putin also used a series of historical parallels and comparisons in order to justify the annexation:

(20) **Let me remind you that in the course of political consultations on the unification of East and West Germany,** at the expert, though very high level, some nations that were then and are now Germany's allies did not support the idea of unification. **Our nation, however, unequivocally supported the sincere, unstoppable desire of the Germans for national unity. I am confident that you have not forgotten this, and I expect that the citizens of Germany will also support the aspiration of the Russians, of historical Russia, to restore unity.**

(21) Moreover, the Crimean authorities referred to the well-known **Kosovo precedent** – a precedent our western colleagues created with their own hands in a **very similar situation**, when they agreed that the unilateral separation of Kosovo from Serbia, exactly what Crimea is doing now, was legitimate and did not require any permission from the country's central authorities.

In the discourse of the statement on the recognition of Abkhazia and South Ossetia the topos of history was used only once, in the context of the comparison between the events of 2008 and 1991:

(22) That **was not the first attempt to do this.** In 1991, President Gamsahourdia of Georgia, having proclaimed the motto "Georgia for Georgians" – just think about it! – ordered attacks on the cities of Sukhum and Tskhinval. The result then was thousands of killed people, dozens of thousands of refugees and devastated villages. And it was Russia who at that time put an end to the eradication of the Abkhaz and Ossetian peoples.

Democracy

The *topos of democracy* and the *argumentum ad populum* were used in both analyzed texts and the manner of using them was quite similar in both cases. Both Putin and Medvedev referred to the results of referendums in order to justify their decisions. However, the percentage of paragraphs devoted to these topoi was larger in the case of Medvedev's speech.

Here are some examples from the statement of 2008:

(23) **The peoples of South Ossetia and Abkhazia have several times spoken out at referendums in favor of independence for their republics.**

(24) The Presidents of South Ossetia and Abkhazia, **based on the results of the referendums conducted and on the decisions**

taken by the Parliaments of the two republics, appealed to Russia to recognize the state sovereignty of South Ossetia and Abkhazia. The Federation Council and the State Duma voted in support of those appeals.

A decision needs to be taken based on the situation on the ground. Considering the **freely expressed will of the Ossetian and Abkhaz peoples** and being guided by the provisions of the UN Charter, the 1970 Declaration on the Principles of International Law Governing Friendly Relations Between States, the CSCE Helsinki Final Act of 1975 and other fundamental international instruments, I signed Decrees on the recognition by the Russian Federation of South Ossetia's and Abkhazia's independence.

The examples of the same topoi can be found in the Crimean Speech:

(25) A referendum was held in Crimea on March 16 in full compliance with democratic procedures and international norms.

More than 82 percent of the electorate took part in the vote. Over 96 percent of them spoke out in favour of reuniting with Russia. These numbers speak for themselves.

(26) The most recent **public opinion surveys** conducted here in Russia show that 95 percent of people think that Russia should protect the interests of Russians and members of other ethnic groups living in Crimea – 95 percent of our citizens.

(27) A total of 86 percent of our people see Crimea as still being Russian territory and part of our country's lands. And one particularly important figure, which corresponds exactly with the result in Crimea's referendum: almost 92 percent of our people support Crimea's reunification with Russia.

(28) Thus we see that the **overwhelming majority of people in Crimea and the absolute majority of the Russian Federation's people support the reunification of the Republic of Crimea and the city of Sevastopol with Russia.**

As one can see, in the Crimean case the president referred not only to the results of the referendum, but also to the survey data in order to justify the claim that Russian citizens want to accept Crimea as a part of Russia.

Conclusions

The comparative analysis of the sets of topoi used in the statement on recognition of Abkhazia and South Ossetia and in the Crimean Speech leads to the following conclusions:

1. The statement on the recognition of South Ossetia and Abkhazia is largely based on the topos of danger.
2. The Crimean Speech is dominated by both the topos of history and the topos of danger.
3. The topoi of rightness and intuition as well as those of language and diversity are used only in the Crimean Speech.
4. The topos of reason is unique to the discourse of recognition of Abkhazia and South Ossetia.
5. The topoi of ethnicity and law are actively used in both texts.
6. For the discourse about South Ossetia and Abkhazia, the topoi of peace, humanitarianism and democracy are also important.

These results can be interpreted from two perspectives. First, they can be seen as evidence of the fact that Russia's policies towards Crimea and towards the secessionist republics in Georgia are not identical. It is not only the formally recognized statuses of these entities that are different, but also the discourse of legitimization of those statuses. The analysis shows that the separation of South Ossetia and Abkhazia are mostly represented as *compelled* secessions, legitimized by a threat, while in the Crimean case one of the main additional discursive motives is that of a *voluntary* secession of an entity that is historically meant to be with Russia.

Second, the comparison of the two texts is also illustrative of Russia's regime drift from 2008 to 2014. From this point of view, the difference between the two texts can be seen as a symptom of a larger discursive shift from the more pragmatic political discourse of 2000s to a more irrational and mythologized discourse of 2010s, i.e. from the formal respect to democratic procedures, law, reason and humanitarian values to the rise of sacralized historical narratives and emotionally charged intuitions.

This trend shows that today Russia is still haunted by the Soviet past and is still influenced by the trauma of the collapse of the USSR and the following period of social disorder. It turns out that the two decades after the collapse of the Soviet empire were not enough to deal with this experience without spiraling back to the heavily ideological discourses.

Sporne secesje ery postsowieckiej w rosyjskim dyskursie politycznym

Praca ma na celu pokazanie, jak secesja Osetii Południowej, Abchazji i Krymu w czasach post-sowieckich jest ujmowana w oficjalnym rosyjskim dyskursie politycznym. Wszystkie trzy powyższe regiony zostały uznane przez Rosję, ale mają one inny status. Abchazja i Osetia Południowa zostały uznane za odrębne państwa, ale nie zostały w pełni włączone do Rosji (chociaż Osetia Południowa kilkakrotnie występowała z taką prośbą), podczas gdy Krym stał się częścią Rosji niemal natychmiast po oddzieleniu się od Ukrainy. Artykuł pokazuje, że nie tylko formalny status tych podmiotów jest inny, lecz dyskurs związany z uznaniem Osetii Południowej i Abchazji za osobne państwa różni się również od tego dotyczącego Krymu. Badania zostały oparte na analizie porównawczej dwóch tekstów: 1) Oświadczenia Dmitrija Miedwiediewa w sprawie uznania Abchazji i Osetii Południowej (26 sierpnia 2008 r.), 2) Przemówienia Władimira Putina dotyczącego Krymu (18 marca 2014 r.). Analiza pokazuje, że casus Osetii Południowej i Abchazji jest najczęściej reprezentowany jako secesja *wymuszona*, podczas gdy w przypadku Krymu jednym z głównych motywów dyskursywnych jest *dobrowolna* secesja półwyspu, który historycznie jest częścią Rosji. Porównanie to ilustruje również sposób, w jaki rosyjskie władze w latach 2008–2014 zmieniały nastawienie do problematycznego dziedzictwa sowieckiej polityki terytorialnej.

Оспариваемые постсоветские сецессии в российском политическом дискурсе[3]

Цель работы показать, как в постсоветское время в официальном российском политическом дискурсе представляется захват Южной Осетии, Абхазии и Крыма. Все три вышеуказанных региона признаны Россией, но имеют разный статус. Абхазия и Южная Осетия считаются скорее отдельными государствами и не были присоединены к России, хотя Южная Осетия (неоднократно обращалась с такими просьбами), в это время как Крым почти сразу после его отделения от Украины стал частью России. В статье показывается, что не только отличается формальный статус этих субъектов, но и дискурс, связанный с признанием Южной Осетии и Абхазии как отдельных государств, отличается от дискурса признания Крыма. Исследование было основано на сравнительном анализе двух текстов: 1) заявления Дмитрия Медведева о признании Абхазии и Южной Осетии (26 августа 2008 года), 2) выступления Владимира Путина посвященного Крыму (18 марта 2014 года). Анализ показывает, что казус Южной Осетии и Абхазии чаще всего представляется как вынужденное отделение, а в случае Крыма одним из главных мотивов дискурса является добровольное отделение полуострова от Украины, который исторически всегда был частью России. Это сравнение также иллюстрирует то, как российские власти в 2008-2014 годах изменили свое отношение к проблемному наследию советской территориальной политики.

[3]   Проект осуществлен при финансовой поддержке Национального научного центра Польши (проект No. 2015/19/B/HS5/02516).

DOI: 10.12797/9788376389042.05

JOACHIM DIEC ⓘD https://orcid.org/0000-0002-3335-3772
Jagiellonian University, Kraków

Chapter 4

A Revolution That Has Not Happened: The Potential of the Russian Nationalist Revival

Introductory remarks

World history abounds with revolutionary political changes. What does not seem important about that topic is the theoretical framework, which allows many scholars to discuss whether a political series of events can be put into the conceptual, systemic framework of "revolution" or not. What is widely accepted among theoreticians is the conviction that a revolution is a radical and anti-systemic political change. The theoretical understanding of revolution is related to the legitimacy of authority. The Weberian tradition includes 3 types of authority: traditional, legal-rational, and charismatic (comp. the critical remarks of Blau, 1963). According to it, a revolution can either violently break the people's readiness to obey commands of a culturally rooted power or overthrow the old regime by acting according to a new system of laws, which replaces the previous one without a sense of remorse. The new leaders and their style can often be defined as charismatic but theoretically we can easily think of a new, even more charismatic avant-garde, which steals the show: in revolutions a more radical kind of modernity usually replaces the previous style, which is perceived to be not revolutionary enough. In other words, revolutions undermine the base of all the three types of authority.

However, what really matters is the fact that after a revolution one's smaller or bigger world will never be the same. Revolutions are incongruent with Tancredi's (a character of Lampedusa's *Leopard*) conviction that "For everything to stay the same, everything must change". After a revolution not too many things stay the same: the main imperatives are either denied or even reversed – what was a vice in the old times becomes a virtue nowadays.

From the empirical or historical perspective, one can observe several types of revolutions. A classical study on the topic, Tanter & Midlarsky (1967, p. 265), lists four types: a mass revolution, a revolutionary coup, a reform coup and a palace revolution. This point of view, however, focuses on the technical aspect of change, whereas in the present study it is much more important to emphasize the object of contestation on the one hand, and the general objective, the imaginary future on the other. From the perspective of the first aspect, a lot of types can be distinguished but most of them boil down to three categories.

1. Some revolutions are generally directed against a monarchy or another kind of autocratic power. Most European revolutions, including the Puritan Revolution in England, the French Revolution and the February Revolution in Russia led to toppling the contested monarchy. The imperatives that lead the revolutionaries to the barricades consist mainly in such things as the elevation of the people or administrative liberalization.

2. When the "people's regime" turns out to be more invasive than the old system, especially if the leftist rules are imposed from

outside, an anti-socialist or an anti-communist revolution may demolish the radically egalitarian authorities. This is the case of the Thermidorian Reaction or the Autumn of Nations in Eastern Europe.

3. Another type of revolution is directed against the state that does not allow a people to develop its nationalistic desires: the will to unite, the desire for the fulfillment of pride, the *libido dominandi* among other nations or, finally, the desire to keep one's own *uniqueness*, which is expressed in Russian with the term of *samobytnost' (самобытность)*. Historically, national revolutions and uprisings have taken various shapes such as the activities of the Spanish Falanga, which successfully fought the internationalist Republic, the Nazi upheaval in the 1930s or the Kurdish revival in Iraq in the 2010s. The theoretical aspect of the topic may not have been studied sufficiently; however, some publications concerning the issue are recommended (Unwalla, 2015; Kumar, 2015).

Russia can be described as a post-revolutionary country in at least two aspects. It underwent a deep deconstruction of its original civilizational structure after 1917 and, after more than 70 years of the communist experiment, it had to face the collapse of the "red empire" and try to build a democratic civil society and free market. As in the case of gnostic utopia and in international relations both at home and abroad, we have to deal with two acts of deconstruction, where old values and dichotomies were replaced by new ones. Old Russia was predominantly an Orthodox and East-Slavic, ethnically Russian (*russkaya*) domain. The most typical oppositions in the political discourse oscillated around two topics:

1. "Russian" versus "Western", where for the Westerners Russia should approach the European standards or, according to the Slavophil thinkers, it should protect its uniqueness and avoid the poison of the Western spirit.

2. "Orthodox" versus "atheist or heretic". For traditionalists and
the vast majority of the Russian population participation in the
Eastern Church was a *sine qua non* condition of being a "real
Russian".

What seems surprising, in spite of the fact that the social
question – the situation of the people – was widely discussed by
the intelligentsia and a kind of "state populism" was also present,
it would not be relevant to say that the intellectual elite tried to
set one of the social classes against the other. Contrary to the
Marxist belief in class struggle, the Russian intelligentsia tried to
be sympathetic toward the peasants and took many actions which
varied from charity to political terror against the state officials
(comp. Nahirny, 1983).

The Bolshevik Revolution of 1917 changed a lot in the narrative.
In fact it became entirely deconstructed. The opposition between
the West and traditional Russia disappeared to be replaced by
another juxtaposition: nationalism (or Great Russian chauvinism
even) versus socialist internationalism. Only political tactics made
Vladimir I. Lenin support the national independence ambitions.
According to the Bolshevik leader, severe steps against nationalisms
would provoke the nations to abandon the only sensible objective
which is the liberalization of the world proletariat. The nations,
focusing on the national conflicts, could thus be successfully tempted
by the exploiters to forget about the main task (Lenin, 1972; see
also the study on the controversy about the issue in Löwy, 1976).

The clue to the problem lies in the fact that before 1917
the value of national patriotism among the opposition was
a positive option, and Western cosmopolitism was perceived as
a problematic attitude (in most of the Russian press and in the
educational narrative; for the leftist intelligentsia the destruction
of the old regime and the old cultural paradigm was the main
objective), whereas now resorting to Russian national sentiments
was proclaimed reactionary and became the negative pole of the

new opposition. As mentioned above, Russian traditionalists glorified the Russian people, especially the peasantry, no less than the leftists did. The goal was different, of course, because the leftists aimed at the liberalization of the "dark mass" and the monarchists, Slavophiles or Pan-Slavists preached about the people as the solid foundation of tsarism and Orthodoxy. Nonetheless, the people and the elite (both reactionary and revolutionary) could agree on a certain kind of solidarity.

The revolution brought about a significant change, which, on a side note, was predicted by the Populist (*Narodnik*) and Bolshevik narratives, where the category of "the enemy of the people" played an important part. Previously, everybody praised the people, now the population was categorized into two different groups: the proletariat, the avant-garde of the proletariat (the Bolshevik Party), and, finally, the group of the enemies of the people. The term became very broad due to the fact that the Bolsheviks (or radical revolutionaries in general) did not enjoy general support. In the election to the Constituent Assembly in late fall of 1917 the socialist agrarian democrats – the Socialist Revolutionary Party with Victor Chernov at the helm won most of the votes in the house, whereas the Bolsheviks with the Left SRs did not even exceed a quarter of the general vote (comp. Radkey, 1950).

The other reason for the expansion of the category was the intention to wipe out not only the reactionary camp but also the left side of the political stage in all cases of real or imaginary disobedience. The Bolsheviks accused the other Russian revolutionaries, the Mensheviks or the Left SRs, of not being revolutionary enough and leading the people astray. The Bolshevik radicalism in the struggle for the ultimate dictatorship of the proletariat turned all the other leftists into the category of the enemy of the people. Moreover, under the Stalin regime many devoted Bolshevik activists were executed as a result of the same kind of accusations (see Stalin's pamphlet: Mastering Bolshevism).

After more than seven decades, the great change of the 1990s brought about another kind of deconstruction. In fact it fits quite well in Tanter & Midlarsky's category of a "reform coup". After December 1991, the Russian people woke up in a different reality: not only had the peaceful revolution destroyed their big state but it also undermined the paradigm of social and moral values. The new times created new oppositions such as

- "democracy" versus "communist authoritarianism",
- "liberalism" versus "Soviet totalitarianism",
- "the self-made person" versus a collectivist "*Homo Sovieticus*" (*совок*).

The axiological values of the poles were reversed: communism was now associated with the lack of personal freedom, the Soviet state was accused of crimes and, consequently, being a *Homo Sovieticus* became an insult (see the study on the *совок* syndrome in Gogin, 2012). The older generation, which was deeply permeated with the idea of economic equality and social security could not understand foreign ideas and imperatives, which forced them to accept aggressive business games, spectacular careers of cunning swindlers, and painful pauperization of the majority of the citizens.

Seeking elements that were commonly present or absent in the axiological oppositions of the three periods mentioned above, one can realize that Post-Communist Russia was unexpectedly quite liberal in the economic sense. Individual freedom and private initiative turned out to be capable of subordinating the other needs and values. The common good, especially in the sense of the social security of the average citizen, was entirely forgotten. In the same way one of the most important triggers for ideologists was lost: the "just cause" or sacrifice in the name of the people. The tsarist doctrine, created in the 1830s by the Minister of National Education, count Sergei Uvarov, promoted the ideas of Orthodoxy (*православие*), Autocracy (*самодержавие*), and, surprisingly enough – *народность*, which can be translated as Nationhood or Peoplehood (Uvarov, 1832). On the other hand, the revolutionary and moderate intelligentsia was ready for jail or hard work in Siberia if their struggle for the happiness of the people demanded such dramatic decisions.

Nothing like that characterizes the latest period of Russian history. Even though the new elite that came to power with Vladimir Putin after the beginning of the new millennium became much more assertive and rejected the previous subordination to Western interests and naive liberalism, it only replaced the previous oligarchy and still avoided any commitments concerning the common good of the citizens. In this way the axiological base of Post-Soviet Russia owes a lot to radical revolutionary deconstruction: it moved away from obligations concerning the people. The new times appeared to be painfully real, they brought about a completely new reality, an odd kind of business-like social contract (Gallopin, 2009).

A historical study concerning any country or civilization ought to be based on facts and keep clear of "the alternative past". In other words, historians describe facts and search for reasons. Political science, however, is not obliged to keep these standards since it is supposed to deal with current events and be confined to prognostic tasks. That is why it has to take into consideration probability and potentials in the same way as facts. Historians (despite being aware of their tasks) may not realize that their vision of the course of events is slightly deterministic whereas in fact none of the recorded and described historical events was entirely predictable *a priori*.

Sudden revolutions as well as longitudinal periods of duration are embedded in a complex structure of conditions, possibilities and decisions. Decisions made either by the leaders or by the people can be studied *a posteriori* but cannot be predicted with absolute certainty. However, the probability of events may be considered while studying the well-known elements of the decision-making process and even ought to be taken into account in a prognostic study (Spetzler and Stael Von Holstein, 1975). Theoretically, our point of interest lies in possible revolutions or other series of events which could have happened, may happen or should happen because of some reasons.

The range of perceived probability can vary from "absolute impossibility" to the strong feeling that "something is in the air" and that we are supposed to experience political turbulence tomorrow. What has to be remembered is the fact that we are still dealing with *perceived* probability since probability in the mathematical or physical sense (in quantum mechanics) cannot be applied directly in political science analyses even if they are based on quantitative (e.g. statistical) research. This does not mean that hard data that are helpful in the explanation of some events such as the number of guns or aircrafts should not be valued. The problem probably lies in the infinite number of conditioning factors.

The present chapter is devoted to an "imaginary revolution", a vital problem in the Russian political reality, which has manifested itself several times but never resulted in a mass uprising or in a reform coup. The topic is somewhat inspired by the considerations of Tat'yana and Valeri Solovei, whose brilliant and pessimistic study *Несостоявшаяся революция* (*The Unfulfilled Revolution*) published in 2011 paints a picture of the tragedy of the Russian nation within its own state and the story of a necessary change that could never be realized because of internal contradictions within the nationalistic camp.

The question of a nationalist revolution in Russia has been widely discussed not only by intellectuals but also among Russian politicians and in the media. In 2005 Andrei Savelyev, a prominent politician and member of the Rodina faction, openly declared in his lecture presented at the St. Petersburg Patriotic Forum that his party was not preparing a revolution but was getting ready for it (Савельев, 2005).

The hypothetical revolutionary option is treated by some circles as necessary because of the impossibility to realize the Russian national idea in a legal way. One of the very few nationalistic parties in Russia which work legally and enjoy their participation in the establishment is the Liberal-Democratic Party of Russia (LDPR) with Vladimir Volfovich Zhirinovsky (Eidelstein) at the helm. However, his program and everyday narrative can be explained as a certain kind of "franchised nationalism" since Zhirinovsky managed to register his party in the Communist era as the Liberal-Democratic Party of the Soviet Union; before that he co-headed the cultural organization Shalom, which was created to channel Jewish sentiments in the situation of increasing anti-Communist attitudes among that minority, which in turn led to mass migration, predominantly to Israel.

Another case of a legal nationalist-conservative political being is the Rodina (Homeland) Party, created in 2003 by Dmitry Rogozin. The party disappeared in 2006 because of a merge with Just Russia but was re-established in 2011 as an outcome of a conference of another nationalist organization: the Congress of Russian Communities. It was initially founded (in 1990) to promote the interests of ethnic Russians who were left beyond the Russian border as a result of the collapse of the USSR. The organization was officially registered in 2011.

The other nationalistic groups, however, were much less successful. The list below illustrates only some representative cases.

1. A relatively early creation – the National-Republican Party of Russia, founded in 1991 by Nikolai Lysenko, was not persecuted as a whole but its leader was charged with the organization of a terrorist attack in the State Duma. Although the accusation was finally rejected, Lysenko was found guilty of stealing a state computer. In 1996, after the arrest of Lysenko, the party split into two factions. The faction which was led by Yuri Belyaev was

later transformed into The Party of Liberty (Партия свободы). Since the National-Republican Party of Russia could not be re-registered until the end of 1998, it practically ceased to exist.

2. The Russian National Unity (Русское Национальное Единство) movement, a relatively big radical and militaristic group, established in 1990 by Alexandr Barkashov, was banned after supporting the Parliament in 1993 and has since been functioning in this manner. The organization tried to take part in the elections of 1999 within the Spas bloc but the Moscow court did not recognize its registration. From that point onwards it has been functioning in a semi-legal capacity. In some interpretations the RNU, the Slavic Union and other organizations of that kind should be described as post-fascist (or post-Nazi even) rather than nationalistic in the classical western tradition of the term (comp. Hearst, 1999).

3. The Union of Orthodox Banner-Bearers (Союз православных хоругвеносцев), which, in fact, is not a political party but an organization founded in 1992 with the goal of re-establishing absolute Christian monarchy, was not banned but had to face several court cases. Its slogan, "Orthodoxy or Death", was removed from a church building near St. Petersburg as a result of the prosecutor's inquiry.

4. The People's National Party (Народная национальная партия), registered originally in 1994 as the Movement of the People's Nationalists (Движение народных националистов), proposed a racist program in which the bloodline conditions the predominance of the Russian nation in the state. The political line of the leader, Alexandr Ivanov-Sukharevsky, as well as that of some other activists, led to the decision about the refusal to re-register the party in 1998.

5. An anti-immigrant nationalistic group – the Movement Against Illegal Immigration, which appeared in 2002 after an ethnic fight between Russians and Armenians in Krasnoarmeysk,

was officially banned by the court in 2011. The movement was originally led by Vladimir Basmanov, then by his brother, Alexandr Belov (Potkin), and, since 2011, by Vladimir Yermolaev. In October 2016 the movement's most influential leader – Alexandr Belov was sentenced to 7.5-year imprisonment in a collective labor colony.

6. The Slavic Union (Славянский союз), organized by Dmitry Demushkin in 2000 concentrated on the idea of an ethnically Russian nation-state. Clear links to some Nazi symbols (the acronym of the organization's name – SS or a kind of swastika) and Holocaust denial made the ban on the organization inevitable: the decision was made by the court in April 2010. After that Demushkin (accompanied by some other activists e.g. Belov-Potkin) decided to take part in the creation of a new organization – The Russians (Русские). However, this one was banned as well in October 2015. Demushkin was put under the travel ban whereas Vladimir Basmanov was forced to go abroad where he created a new nationalistic group: the Committee "Nation and Liberty" (Комитет «Нация и Свобода»).

7. The national-traditionalist Great Russia Party (Великая Россия), founded by Dmitry Rogozin and Andrei Savelyev in 2007 was refused registration twice, which led to a temporary break in its functioning. However, in 2010 another attempt to re-establish the party was made.

8. The National-Democratic Party (Национально-Демократическая Партия), which was created by Konstantin Krylov in 2012 on the base of two organizations: the Russian Social Movement (Русское Общественное Движение) and the Russian Civic Union (Русский Гражданский Союз), was officially registered in 2014 but later the registration information was refuted. Krylov himself was put on trial under Article 282 of the infamous bill of 2002 in connection with his public speech at the rally – "Stop feeding the Caucasus", held on October 22, 2011 at Bolotnaya Square in Moscow,

and sentenced to 120 hours of correctional labor, which made him legally unable to become the official leader of any party (Tipaldou, 2015, p. 70).

This short overview suffices to reveal the range of Russo-centric nationalist sentiments in the Russian Federation. The main question, however, is about the reasons for the appearance of Russian nationalism nowadays in the country where the most important positions belong to ethnic Russians and where the widely promoted Russian language and culture are supposed to shape the behavioral patterns of the population. Two options seem the most obvious at first sight: the historical grounds – the soil for a possible nationalist change, or the current situation, which may have led the Russian nation to take such steps.

The traditions of Russian nationalism

From a theoretical point of view, we must be aware that there are various kinds of nationalism, and that Russia is by no means an exception: the term of nationalism can be applied there to phenomena which are conceptually far from each other. We may consider various typologies. For example, Hechter (2000) suggests such kinds of nationalism as:

- **state-building nationalism**, whose essence lies in creating a more homogenous society,
- **peripheral nationalism**, found in communities which try to avoid acculturation,
- **irredentist nationalism**, with a tendency to enlarge the state's territory,
- **unification nationalism**, which "involves the merger of a politically divided but culturally homogeneous territory into one state" (Hechter, 2000, pp. 15–17).

In fact we could also distinguish some other forms, such as the ethnic, cultural, political, nativistic or vitalistic kind of nationalism

(Bäcker, 2008, pp. 11ff). The general question probably lies in the definition of *la nation*, which generally boils down to three essentially different bases: **the ethnic (or racial) root, culture** and **statehood**. However, it seems that it is the empirical material that delivers some more convincing hints for structuring the tradition of nationalism in Russia.

At any rate, in order to attempt to clarify the structure of conditioning circumstances one has to look back to the traditions of Russian nationalism according to the shape they have taken in Russian historiography and in the classical works describing the history of Russian political thought. Nationalism in Russia is by no means an invention of the end of the 20th century. It generated several earlier incarnations. Here are the most representative ones:

1. Slavophilism (slavyanofil'stvo, славянофильство), which was originally constructed by a very small group of columnists such as Ivan Kireevsky, Konstantin Aksakov, Alexei Khomyakov or Yuri Samarin. The movement's thinkers preached about the superiority of Orthodoxy – the only true religion, the historical tradition of Old Rus' and the Eastern conciliarism over the Western legacy: the intellectualism of Western Christianity, the tradition of competition, social contract and papalism. The Slavophiles, who strongly criticized the Petrine reforms, were not the beloved child of the court, which made itself out to be a reliable and modern European monarchy rather than a museum of medieval folk culture (comp. Walicki, 1975).

2. Pochvennichestvo (почвенничество), which was a philosophy of the return to the roots, a trend that appeared among traditionalist publishers, critics and writers such as Apollon Grigoryev, Nikolai Strakhov or Fyodor Dostoevsky. The pochvenniks did not reject modernization but emphasized the necessity to cultivate Russian convictions, especially the ones that referred to Orthodox practices and national axiology (comp. Walicki, 1975).

3. Russian Pan-Slavism – the idea of uniting all Slavs. The trend began in the Austrian Empire but was soon taken over by Russian ideologists such as Mikhail Pogodin, Nikolai Y. Danilevsky, Ivan Aksakov, Vladimir Cherkassky, Rostislav Fadeev. The main ideological base for the doctrine was formulated by Danilevsky in his famous book *Russia and Europe* (Eng. trans. 2013), where he introduced the idea of a Slavic Union with the capital in Constantinople, which was supposed to be regained from the Turks (comp. MacMaster, 1967; Snyder, 1984, pp. 17–36).

4. The Black Hundred (Чёрная сотня) ideologies, which were represented by several organizations such as the Union of the Russian People (Союз русского народа), Russian Monarchist Party (Русская монархическая партия), White Two-Headed Eagle (Белый двуглавый орёл) or St. Michael's Union (Русский Народныи Союз имени Святого Михаила Архангела), established by the famous and controversial activist Vladimir Purishkevich. Their programs, which were in fact a reaction to socialist and liberal movements, included such elements as devotion to the throne and Orthodox religion, anti-socialism, anti-Westernism, various forms of anti-Semitism including anti-assimilationism, and the conviction that building a nation state is a necessity (comp. Laqueur, 1993).

What may be surprising nowadays is the fact that modern Russian nationalism, although it is equally suppressed and marginalized as it was under the tsarist regime, does not descend from the old doctrines apart from the most basic idea that constitutes any nationalism – the elevation of the nation. The only visible convergence can be observed between modern Russian nationalism and the Black Hundreds. How can that be explained? Paradoxically, this historical reflection takes us to another line of explanation: to facts and numbers.

The ethnic and social reality after the Russian Revolution

What made the situation after 1905 in Russia under the old regime different from the last decades of the former century was the fact that the traditionalistic and nationalist circles realized that at that time not only a narrow elite but also a significant part of the working class, including the peasantry, which made up no less than 85% of the whole population, felt disappointed with the regime and was ready to promote significant reforms. The contestation of the emperor's court as well as of the church, which provided strong ideological support to the throne, made the Russian rightists aware that the spirit began to shift to the left. But was it simply a turn in the Russian soul?

The Russian Empire had never been a national state. As already mentioned, it was only ideologically integrated by the values of Orthodoxy, Authority and Peoplehood. The monarchs had no Russian blood in their veins, and many high-ranking officials were either foreigners or people of non-Russian descent. However, the 19th century brought about extraordinary interest in foreign social and political ideas. Moreover, some important political movements were created with significant presence of Jewish, Polish and other activists who represented various nations, which were by no means interested in the stability of the empire.

The importance of that issue can be illustrated by pure facts. The non-Marxist revolutionary Populist (*Narodnik*) organizations, which caused the original political unrest, owed a lot to people of foreign descent. Among the very few founders of the Black Repartition (Черный передел) there are such figures as Paul Axelrod and Leo Deutsch, who were born into Jewish families. In the more radical and terrorist faction Narodnaya Volya (People's Will) one should not forget the names of Yakov Yudelevsky, a Belarusian Jew and a significant French philosopher, as well as the figure of the Polish nobleman Ignacy Hryniewiecki, the killer of tsar Alexander II. One of the most prominent theoreticians of Russian socialism was Vasily (Vilgelm) Bervi-Flerovsky, son of William Bervy, an official of the Ministry of Justice of purely English descent. The theoreticians of legal Marxism: Nikolai Sieber and Petr Struve had well-known German ancestors; Struve was a grandson of a famous astronomer, Friedrich Georg Wilhelm von Struve. The Menshevik leaders were predominantly Jewish with Yulius Martov (Tsederbaum) at the helm. Vladimir I. Lenin, the leader of the Bolshevik faction, had Russian but also many other roots. His father was of Russian, Chuvash and Mordvin (or Kalmyk) descent whereas his mother had Swedish, German, Russian as well as Jewish ancestors. A brief look at the other prominent leaders of the party explains a lot: Leo Trotsky (Leiba Bronstein), Lev Kamenev (Rosenfeld), Grigory Zinoviev (Hirsch Apfelbaum) and Lazar Kaganovich were unquestionably Jewish, Joseph Stalin (Dzhugashvili), Sergo Ordzhonikidze and Lavrentiy Beria were Georgian, Anastas Mikoyan – Armenian; the founder of Cheka – Feliks Dzerzhinsky (Feliks Dzierżyński) – a Polish nobleman, whereas the most radical activist of that institution and the head of the Red Army Cheka, Martin Lacis (Jānis Sudrabs) – a Latvian farmworker.

The feeling that citizens of foreign descent (rus. inorodcy, инородцы) were predominantly responsible for the destruction of the empire was strengthened by the ethnic structure of Russia, which evolved throughout the passing decades. Before the partitions of Poland (1772, 1793 and 1795) the Russian territory was settled mainly by Eastern Slavs. The tiny minorities, such as the Finno-Ugric peoples or Tartars did not play a big part in the country's policies. However, after the annexation of a significant part of Poland and the Napoleonic Wars, the Russian Empire began to grow again and absorbed numerous and "problematic" nations. The much better educated and technologically advanced

Poles gradually became more and more hostile toward the regime and to Russia in general. At the end of the 19th century the Jewish population, which became a "blessing" after the incorporation of Poland's eastern territories, began to take active part in the revolutionary movement since its position in the empire was quite far from modern standards of civic equality. What seemed especially annoying to some Jews was the Pale of Settlement (cherta osedlosti, черта оседлости) proclaimed in a decree issued by Catherine the Great in 1791. According to the decree, which was later annexed by the bill of 1804, Jews could only settle in the Western territories of the empire in sixteen governorates. The other problem was the lack of political rights until the last days of the tsarist state. It was apparent that Russian Jews hoped for suffrage in the new form of the country; in a way their hopes came true after 1917.

In the second half of the 19th century the country experienced another inflow of ethnically non-Russian citizens (or, to be precise, subjects to the emperor) – the Muslim peoples of Central Asia, which at that time was usually named Turkestan. Russia's expansion to the South was unwillingly directed to the Islamic and Turkic world. Initially, the people of Turkestan – Kazakhs, Uzbeks, the Kyrgyz people, Iranian Tajiks – did not seem a real challenge. Their demographic dynamics were not too impressive since the Orthodox and Slavic part of the population developed faster.

According to the first imperial census, which was held in 1897, Russia was inhabited by 126.5 million people. Orthodox and Old-Believer Christians amounted to more or less 109.1 million, which comprised 86.2% of the population, Roman Catholics – 11.5 million (9%), Jews – 5.2 million (4%), Muslims – 13.9 million (10.9%) (Демоскоп, № 741–742). Although the numbers draw a picture of a multi-cultural empire, the burden of the Southern, Western and Eastern frontiers did not seem too heavy for the vigorous and well-developing "state-forming nation" – ethnic Russians.

The territory of the Soviet Union after World War II was almost of the same size. Moscow only gave up the east-central Polish provinces. After the 1989 census it was possible to make some conclusions about the demographic tendencies in the last decade. It turned out that the dynamics were generally positive. However, some nations grew much more than others if one compares the results to those of the previous census, which was held in 1979. The main nation was still on its way up: in 10 years it managed to reach a 6% growth whereas Poles or Jews recorded a decline (98% and 76% respectively). However, there was a tendency that had continued for more than two decades: the fast growth of the Muslim nations such as the Uzbeks (34%), Chechens (27%), Turkmen people (35%), Kazakhs (24%), Azeri people (24%), Tajik people (45%), Ingush people (28%) and Avars (24%) (Лабутова, 1990).

These data might have caused some reflection but in fact they were ignored at that time since the main topic of intellectual disputes was strictly political and concerned the reforms that were supposed to revitalize the USSR as a whole. In 1991 the "red empire" collapsed, which correctly seemed to be the main issue. Moscow lost direct control over nearly a quarter (23.77%) of the territory of the USSR. Theoretically the Russian republic, now liberated from the non-Russian rest, should have created the best conditions for the development of the Russian nation. The coming decades brought about a colossal demographic disaster and a visible change of proportions of the particular ethnic groups (comp. Вишневский, 2016).

According to official data the Russian ethnic group within the territory of the Russian Federation comprised 81.53% of the whole population in 1989. It is in fact a weaker result than the percentage of Orthodox Christians in the Russian empire at the end of the 19th century. In 2010 the index only reached 80.9%. The second ethnic group – the Tartars – enjoyed a growth from 3.76 to 3.87%, whereas the Chechens – a dynamic jump from 0.61

to 1.04, the Ingush people from 0.15 to 0.32 and the Azeri group from 0.23 to 0.44 (in the case of the last two groups the index doubled) (Федеральная служба государственной статистики, 2012, p. 72). According to the data from 2010 the decrease in the ethnic Russian element (if compared to 2002) constituted 4.2 per cent, whereas in the case of the whole population it amounted to only 1.59%. At the same time the increase in the number of Chechens reached 5.23%, of Uzbeks – 135% (166 946 people) and of Kyrgyz people – 225.14%. The inflow of groups which did not determine their nationality was estimated at 285.38% (4 168 678 people) (Statdata, 2017). More recent data are going to be available after the next census.

The official data, although convincing enough, may not reflect the reality. In informal conversations Russian officials express their doubts about the methodology of the last census and are afraid that in reality the demographic situation of the Russian nation might be much gloomier. According to many commentators (whose opinions by no means come from the opposition) the real number of Russians is probably significantly lower, especially if one takes into account the extinction of the provincial areas (вымирание глубинки). In 2017 the analysts of "Realnoye Vremya", apposing the demographic indices of the first halves of 2016 and 2017, discovered that the demographic dynamics in the whole territory of the Russian Federation once again began a catastrophic downfall, especially in Moscow (34.4%). The situation is also not good in Tatarstan. However, there are no indicators whether this concerns the Russian part of the population or rather the Tartars (Реальное Время, 2017).

Although before 2017 the demographic data became slightly more optimistic the nationalistic circles still complained that Russia managed to overcome the most dramatic decline only because the native Russian population had been for years gradually replaced by Muslim incomers from Central Asia and the Northern Caucasus (comp. Царский Путь. Русский Оперативный Журнал, 2017).

The problem is that the real range of this phenomenon is relatively difficult to estimate. According to Marlene Laruelle (2016) the number of Muslims in Russia is about 15 million with one in ten located in Moscow. As she says, "Given forthcoming demographic changes, by around 2050 Muslims will represent between one third (according to the most conservative estimates) and one half (according to the most alarmist assessments) of the Russian population". Laruelle correctly points out the main trends of Moscow's policy toward the growing number of Russian Muslims. Firstly, it emphasizes Russia's openness and friendliness as a peaceful country, based on respect towards traditional religions. Secondly, it rejects radical Islam labeling all non-conformist groups as linked to Wahhabism. Thirdly, it also tries to present itself as a part of the Islamic world, a traditionalistic global power opposed to the "rotten West" (Laruelle, 2016).

This puts the Russian nationalistic circles in an awkward position. Trying to defend "traditional values" they unwillingly place themselves on the side of the Kremlin, which in fact introduces a kind of "creeping revolution", deconstructing the exploited term of "traditional values". There is no doubt that Christianity (including Orthodoxy) does not promote homosexuality and patchwork communities, trying to help traditional families instead. However, the most basic values of Christianity such as charity toward all people or devotion to the truth about the union of God and man in the person of Jesus Christ are incongruent with the Muslim ones. A Christian traditionalist cannot agree with a Muslim traditionalist in the dispute on the number of wives a man may have. The "traditionalists of all countries unite" imperative is a caricature of the Marxist slogan rather than a Christian objective.

The reflection on the two main types of reasons for a possible national revolution in Russia can only lead to a conclusion that the evolving ethnic situation in the contemporary state seems to be a much more important motivator than the traditional models of Russian nationalism, which appeared before the political disaster of 1917. In other words, today's Russian nationalists are not Slavophiles, *почвенники* or Pan-Slavists; they are people who face the challenge of a dying "state nation", even if their obsession is based on a kind of individual fear rather than an analysis of statistical data.

* * *

Keeping in mind the historical and social grounds for a national revolution in Russia we still do not solve the main problem which is the question about the hypothetical possibility of such a change. To open a perspective for some attempts it is necessary to point to such issues as:

- a modern theoretical base that could be convincing for contemporary Russians,
- the organizational potential,
- the political conditions,
- the readiness of the Russian people to understand the ethnic question and appreciate the attempts of the potential revolutionary nationalists, the feeling that something has to be changed.

The theoretical base

Russian nationalism of the recent decades is represented not only by emotional pamphlets; there is also an abundance of important and valuable patterns and theoretical models, which have to be taken into deep consideration. However, not all proposals are widely known and kept in memory, which makes some relatively unproductive. The Russian political and social base of narratives after the Stalin era provides an interesting range of topics. They can be classified in various ways, according to chronological or typological criteria. However, it is obvious that non-communist thought began with the "dissidents", non-conformists of the Khrushchev and Brezhnev era. Some of them, such as Marxist revisionists (representatives of "economism") appeared as a result of intellectual resistance which remained within the Soviet "internationalist" paradigm.

Generally speaking, Russian dissidents of the 1960s and 1970s represented various options. Originally the differences were interpreted in a simplified way: the dissidents were divided into "the lefts" – those who accepted Marxism (or socialism in general) but rejected Stalinism and the rights – those who rejected Marxism completely and were "genuine Russian patriots". They were associated with a critical attitude both to Soviet policies and to the Russian authoritarian past. In fact, "the lefts" such as Andrei Sakharov, Andrei Siniavsky, Grigory Pomerants or Alexandr Yanov did not necessarily stick to Marxism. They simply tried to act in specific conditions. On the other hand, it is definitely true that many of them, such as Yanov, Pomerants or Siniavsky were of Jewish descent, which could make their ideas less popular among ethnic Russians.

The other group was associated with "Slavophilism" since it emphasized the values of the Orthodox tradition as well as the legacy of Old Russia and Russian culture. This group, which ought to be much more in focus in the present study, is associated with such figures as Alexandr Isaevivh Solzhenitsyn, the famous writer and Noble Prize winner, Igor Rostislavovich Shafarevich, a distinguished mathematician, or Vadim Mikhailovich Borisov, whose name is nearly forgotten nowadays. However, it was Borisov who drafted the postulate of Russia's obligation to find its own national face in his text placed in the famous collection *From Under the Rubble* (*Из-под глыб*, 1974, p. 200).

The greatest popularity was originally enjoyed by Solzhenitsyn who created an important pattern of modern and sublime nationalism whose essence boils down to a couple of points:

1. Communism is not a Russian invention. Its idea was imported from the West and implemented by an uprooted elite; it is followed by the new intelligentsia, which in fact lost its contact with the nation (*Из-под глыб*, 1974, pp. 217–260).
2. Russia should not seek inspiration in the West since the latter passively accepts communism and because of its consumerism is unable to struggle for higher values (Солженицын, 1978).
3. Russia should limit its expansionary ambitions and get rid of the Soviet ideology, especially the idea of materialistic progress (Солженицын, 1990).
4. The Russian nation should develop according to the spiritual model of Russian peasantry (Солженицын, 1998).

Solzhenitsyn's ideas, which became popular in the 1980s and 1990s, were quite congruent with the ones proposed by Igor Shafarevich, whose model contained similar postulates:

1. Socialism is an ancient and destructive tendency in the development of humanity. The doctrine was imposed on the Russian people because of a non-native harmful germ (Шафаревич, 1977).
2. Although socialist destruction appeared within the circles of Russian intelligentsia it would have never succeeded if it had not been for the presence of the Jewish element (Шафаревич, 2005, pp. 432–441).
3. The Western intellectual world as well as alienated intellectuals of foreign descent in Russia are permeated with russophobia, which rejects the Russian tradition and ambitions as well as the country's rural heritage (Шафаревич, 1988).

Shafarevich's concept of the Jews and alienated intellectuals as a destructive minority within the big nation (an idea borrowed from Augustin Cochin) still seems to be rather a reflection of Russian nationalism before World War I even though it was exploited within the circles of contemporary nationalists. What became especially productive is the notion of *russophobia*, a term that became popular not only among the right camp activists but also in the narratives applied by Russian officials and governmental spin doctors.

Trying to determine the probability of a national revolution in Russia, one has to consider the model of nationalism which resorts to the Orthodox tradition such as the Union of Orthodox Banner-
-Bearers. However, it must be remembered that its adherents face an unsolvable problem. Since they treat Orthodoxy as the only true faith (единая православная вера) they are obliged to admit its universality. In other words, they cannot "privatize" or "nationalize" their religion, which is a common temptation in many cultural circles: to be a "real" Russian tone ought to be an Orthodox, in the same way a "real" Japanese citizen should be a Shintoist, a "real" Jew – a Judaist, a "real" Englishman – an Anglican, a "real" Pole – a Catholic. This issue becomes problematic while discussing the Ukrainian question since the Ukrainians are predominantly Orthodox but have a strong conviction of being a separate nation.

A relatively odd model of nationalism was presented by the National Bolshevist movement, which took the shape of The National-Bolshevik Front, the National-Bolshevik Party, and (since 2010) of The Other Russia (Другая Россия), a party that was denied registration. Their *spiritus movens* was the scandalous writer Eduard Limonov. The ideology of "nazbols" was a combination of totalitarian communism and fascist nationalism. This trend of Russian nationalist thought was probably a reaction to the liberalization and democratization of Russia that took place in the 1990s. Limonov strongly resisted any kind of liberalism, democracy and capitalism promoting the idea of a strong state led by an authoritarian leader who would defend the interests of the people. In the area of foreign policy the nazbols intended to re-integrate the post-Soviet area and severely suppress the minorities. They identified the main enemy with the US (The National-Bolshevik Party website, 2007).

Another semi-nationalist product of post-Stalinist Russia was neo-Eurasianism, a trend that originated in the interwar time (and was at that point represented by such thinkers as duke Nikolai Trubetzkoy, Petr Savitsky, Petr Suvchinsky, Georgi Florovsky, Lev Karsavin, Dmitry Svyatopolk-Mirsky and Nikolai Alekseev). In the Soviet era it was continued by a highly popular ethnologist – Lev Nikolaevich Gumilyov, the son of famous poets: Anna Akhmatova and Nikolai Gumilyov. Gumilyov suggested that the Russian ethnos is a product of the modern era, not of Old Rus' and that it cultivates the legacy of Genghis-Khan. Consequently, the Russian people represent Eurasian virtues rather than European or Slavic ones. The Eurasian nation is the ethnic substrate of Eurasia, which is generally identical to the territory of the Soviet Union (Гумилев, 2002; Пальцев, 2011).

After the collapse of the USSR the neo-Eurasian idea was popularized by other ideologists with their unquestionable leader – Alexandr Gelevich Dugin. At the beginning of his intellectual journey he proclaimed a "conservative revolution" (a term borrowed from Armin Mohler) after the decades of communism. However, in what is probably his most popular book, Dugin discusses the grounds of geopolitics and develops a strikingly anti-Western theory. He exploits Mackinder's old scheme of the competition between the sea powers and the continental ones. According to Dugin, Russia is the medium of tellurocracy (the continental power), which stands for conservatism/tradition, autocracy and collective responsibility for the economy whereas the Atlantic powers (especially the US and the United Kingdom) represent talassocracy, the power of the sea, which dissolves collective obligations. The Western world proposes progress instead of tradition, democracy and capitalism, the free market, which is responsible for nothing and nobody (Dugin, 1998).

In Dugin's works the Russian nation is not an ethnic being but a Eurasian bedrock of tradition. If we treat neo-Eurasianism as a kind of nationalism, we have to deal with a specific understanding of it. There is no doubt that Dugin delivered an influential model of Great Russia, an "immortal homeland". In this concept the Russian people together with the other ethnic groups (which form the great nation of the Eurasian niche) are responsible for the communitarian and traditionalist ethos. Dugin is devoted to Orthodoxy in a specific sense. In his books and interviews the Russian faith is presented as a "tradition" rather than a "religion", which is normally conditioned by specific rules and beliefs. This way Dugin ignores the differences between Orthodoxy and tribal Islam, and rejects Western Christianity as an intellectual doctrine.

Thus, the neo-Eurasianist concept cannot be categorized only in terms of nationalism. This refers both to the interwar, primary tradition of the movement and to its later forms. Bäcker (2000) describes the development of early Eurasianism as a transition from a kind of reaction against acculturation to totalitarianism; this well-grounded approach seems to be even better justified by today's forms of the movement. According to some recent publications (e.g. Mostafa, 2013) Eurasianism is interpreted as a unifying political program where ethnic nationalisms are replaced by another kind of peaceful solidarity.

Another theoretical model was delivered by the "tribalists" (or racists even), where the nation bears a strictly ethnic meaning, and the underlying principle of nationalism lies in the idea of the purity of blood (usually known in its Iberian variations – the Portuguese *limpeza de sangue* or the Spanish *limpieza de sangre*), in the ties of kinship. This radical point of view was proposed in the founding texts of The People's National Party, in the ideology of the Slavic Union and in the marginal national-socialist groups. One of the most interesting and, at the same time, most consistent visions of the Russian nation's fate was presented by Alexei Shiropayev in his 2001 book *The Prison of the Nation (Тюрьма народа)*, where Russia is illustrated as a place of great sufferings of the

Russian tribe. Shiropaev understands it as an Aryan community which originated in the North-Eastern territories of Europe and descends from Nordic Varangians and Vendens (Slavs). In the course of time the Russian tribe had to face dramatic challenges. The foreign influence – Eastern, Greek Christianity, which in fact originated in the Jewish den, and invasions from the East (the inflow of such peoples as Turkic Pechenegs and Polovtsy, Mongols, Tartars, etc.) subordinated the nation to Eastern rulers, who soon became princes and emperors. Under Soviet rule the Russian tribe was exterminated by Jewish commissars or Asian activists. The Soviet Union led most of the Russian people to death, with the Great Famine in Ukraine and ruthless tactics during World War II (Широпаев, 2001).

Finally, we also have to account for a model which is visibly related to contemporary incarnations of European "defensive" nationalism. Some Russian nationalists make conclusions which are analogous to the ones of the Party for Freedom in Holland, the Alternative for Germany, Pegida or the National Front in France. The model includes mainly the hostility to immigration caused by the fear of a barbarian, predominantly Islamic flood. The most incisive narrative of that sort was presented in the program of the Movement Against Illegal Immigration (DPNI).

However, there is also a much more sophisticated and moderate version of "defensive" or "cultural" nationalism in contemporary Russia, a program which is also widely accepted among many intellectuals. It is connected mainly with the National-Democratic Party and its academic tribune in the form of "Voprosy nacionalizma", an interesting and influential journal in which the questions of the possibility to build or re-create the Russian nation as well as nationalism in general are discussed on a relatively high level. Apart from Krylov, who is the head of the journal, Natalya Kholmogorova – the co-founder of the initiative, Nedezhda Shalimova – the Secretary of the Russian Social

Movement, as well as Sergei Sergeev (Сергеев, 2017a; Сергеев, 2017b), a respected and moderate historian, should also be taken into consideration as the ideological leaders of the trend.

To sum up, we can say that Russia has received a rich and diversified set of models that could be followed by a mass nationalistic movement. However, one should also realize that the exploitation of the theoretical concepts given above sketches a dichotomous explanatory model of Russian nationalism. Its internal divergence was also formulated by Tat'yana and Valerii Solovei, who make a distinction between **the supporters of a purely national state** and **the imperialists** (Соловей and Соловей, 2011, p. 402). Most of Russian nationalists are somewhere in between but the contradiction remains clear: imperialism is an efficient impediment to the perspective of an ethnically pure country. In other words, Russia for Russians would be inevitably smaller than a monstrous Great Russia (*Великая Россия*).

The organizational potential

Russian nationalism is represented by many groups and theoreticians. Most of these circles are (or were) relatively small and often had no real access to peripheral areas. Giving a full picture of nationalist organizations in Russia is hardly possible. Some of them are listed by Dubas (2008, pp. 47ff), some are described in other studies such as Laruelle et al. (2009). The list given below is by no means complete. However, for further studies it is advisable to remember such groups, organizations and parties as:

1. "National traditionalist" organizations:

   Formerly:

   – The Memory (Память, *Pamyat*), the oldest post-Stalinist nationalist organization, which goes back to the beginning of the 1970s and ceased to exist in 2003 after the death of its leader, Dmitry Vasilyev.

   Currently:

   – Great Russia (since 2007).

2. The xenophobic and anti-immigrant ones:
   - Rus – Party for the Defence of the Russian Constitution (Партия Защиты Российской Конституции "Русь", ПЗРК),
   - Russian National Unity (Русское Национальное Единство),
   - The Movement Against Illegal Immigration (Движение Против Нелегальной Иммиграции).
3. Ethnic and racist nationalist groups:
   - The Russian Social Movement (Русское Общественное Движение),
   - The Slavic Union (Славянский Союз),
   - The National Union (Народный Союз),
   - National Socialist Society (Национал-социалистическое общество),
4. The National-Bolshevik organizations:
   Formerly:
   - National Bolshevik Front (1993),
   - National Bolshevik Party (1994–2007).
   Currently:
   - The Other Russia (since 2010).
5. The Orthodox-nationalistic organizations:
   - The Union of Orthodox Banner Bearers (Союз православных хоругвеносцев),
   - The Union of Orthodox Citizens (Союз православных граждан),
   - Radonezh (Радонеж).
6. Eurasianist formations:
   - Eurasia Party (Партия "Евразия"),
   - the Eurasian Youth Union (Евразийский союз молодежи).
7. State nationalist (imperialist) parties and organizations:
   - Liberal-Democratic Party of Russia,
   - "Rodina" Party – The National Front (Партия "РОДИНА"),

- The Congress of Russian Communities (Конгресс русских общин).

The number of the members of the particular groups is difficult to estimate. Even the officially registered establishment organizations and parties do not publish such statistics. However, in 2008 the "Kommersant" magazine, pointing to the information available then in the Federal Registration Bureau (Федеральная регистрационная служба), provided the number of LDPR members which was supposed to be 155.86 thousand ("Коммерсант", 2008). The radical groups are rather small and usually do not exceed 100 activists in each of the centers. The cores of the organizations, however, are surrounded by a changing number of supporters.

What seems to be a valuable source of information (from the organizational perspective) is the demonstration which is annually held on November 4 (the Day of National Unity) – the Russian March. The organizers declare that

> the Russians are dissatisfied with the fact that they do not have their own national state, that their interests are not considered in Russia, because of the adoption of "substituting migration", and because their existence and their right to determine their own future are now being questioned.

The organization of the demonstration is in the hands of the Center for the Russian Committee of the Russian March, which nominally consisted of 9 people in September 2017:

- Vladimir Basmanov – the founder of the anti-immigrant DPNI and of the Russian Association in exile, as well as the head of the "Nation and Freedom" Committee, one of the main organizers of the first Russian March and many subsequent ones,
- Alexandr Belov – his brother, a political prisoner since 2016, one of the leaders of the DPNI and the Russian Association,

another key organizer of the first Russian March and many subsequent ones,

- Maxim Vakhromov – one of the leaders of the National Union of Russia (Национальный Союз России), the leader of the nationalists in Yekaterinburg where he organizes the Russian marches,
- Vitaly Goryunov – one of the leaders of the National Union of Russia, the head of the nationalists of Tula and the organizer of the Russian Marches in Tula,
- Sergey Guzhev – the organizer of the Russian Marches in Vologda,
- Aleksey Kolegov – a political prisoner, one of the leaders of the Russian Association and the organization Frontier of the North (Рубеж Севера), formerly the main organizer of the Russian Marches in Syktyvkar (Komi Republic),
- Georgi Pavlov – the organizer of the Russian Marches in Pskov,
- Igor Stenin – one of the leaders of the Russian Association, the main organizer of the Russian Marches in Astrakhan,
- Alexei Bakhtin – a political prisoner, formerly the main organizer of the Russian Marches in Novosibirsk.

The Central Organizing Committee embraces interregional advisory groups which include all the organizers of the Russian March who would like to take part in the collegial discussion about preparations for the Russian March. There are also a number of functional commissions within the Committee, formed by various participants who devote their time to organizational issues (see Русский марш, 2017).

According to the Agency of Russian Information the number of participants of the march in 2006 exceeded 7000 (Агентство Русской Информации, 2006). The exact data referring to the march in 2016 and 2017 are not available. However, as one of the oldest organizers, Alexei Mikhailov, declared in an interview, after the march he was taken to the local police department

(Управление внутренних дел) and fined because the declared number of participants was exceeded: no fewer than 8 thousand people turned up (Михайлов, 2016). Such numbers (if one takes into account the size of Moscow) do not make a great impression. However, we have to remember that Russian national extremists are under constant control and a gathering such as the Russian March during a national holiday provides evidence for the determination of the nationalistic circles.

Political conditions

There is no doubt that the Russian authorities, both in the 1990s and later, found imperialist and statist nationalism much more suitable for the realization of their objectives than the racist or anti-immigrant versions (comp. Panov, 2010). People like Dmitry Rogozin (who has held the post of Deputy Prime Minister of the Russian Federation since 2011), the leader of Rodina and the Congress of Russian Communities, or Alexandr Dugin, the founder of the neo-Eurasianist movement (who received substantial financial support for his publications and even became the chair of the Sociology of International Relations at Moscow State University), were by no means treated as unwanted people within the Russian political establishment.

Since the imperial nationalists, unlike the liberals, supported the hard line toward the West, especially to the US, the Kremlin, especially after 2000, treated them as natural allies: they at least aimed at the extension of Moscow's influence to former Soviet republics, where a good part of the new states' population was ethnically Russian. The liberals of the 1990s did not see any chance of success in such assertive behavior and highlighted the possible negative consequences, especially in the sphere of international trade.

Putin's regime did a lot to not only get rid of the liberal opposition but also to hamper the budding development of another potential enemy: the radical nationalist non-conformist groups. There were several reasons behind this course of action. First of all, they were difficult to control and resorted to direct public support with no intermediation of the Kremlin. Another problem lay and still lies in their exclusive style: appealing to ethnic Russian sentiments they exclude a large and still growing milieu of nations which were tempted by Putin's regime to unite under the control of Moscow. The Kremlin, as it previously was in the case of the Mongol Empire, Victorian Britain or imperial Russia, appeared to be unable to give up the idea of expansion. In other words, geopolitical imperatives (according to state documents, presidential addresses to the National Assembly and political practice in nearly all spheres) overshadowed the economic, or, more generally, the civilizational ones. Finally, at least some of the nationalistic groups such as the DPNI or People's National Party served programs which matched very well the European practice of extreme nationalism. This way they seemed to be much more pro-European than pro-Eurasian: they discovered that the Russians are white Christians or white Aryans, and that they constitute a part of the European civilization.

The main device used as a weapon in the struggle against the nationalist threat is the refusal to register a party under the pretext of extremism. Since 2002 a significant number of political parties and organizations have been denied registration because of real or imaginary extremism on the grounds of the *Федеральный закон О противодействии экстремистской деятельности*. Chapter 1 of the bill states that extremist activity also includes such things as "incitement to social, racial, ethnic or religious hatred; propaganda of exclusiveness, superiority or inferiority of an individual based on his/her social, racial, ethnic, religious or linguistic identity, or his/her attitude to religion". This way Putin's KGB team obtained a perfect device to eliminate ethnic nationalists from the main game of thrones. Since 2002 a great number of nationalistic organizations and parties were refused registration; some were banned and persecuted.

The Russian state of mind

Russian nationalistic sentiments are not easy to study because the matter is somewhat elusive. However, we can take into consideration the results of the public opinion research conducted by Levada Center in which the respondents were asked about their attitude to the nationalist imperative: "Russia only for Russians". The initial set of studies was done in the years 1998–2009. The results were unclear and did not reveal any unquestionable tendency. Strong support varied from 14% in 2007 to 19% in 2005. Relative support ("it would be advisable to realize this idea in a reasonable framework") ranged from 31% in 1998 to 42% in 2008. Strong objection gained the least popularity (18%) in 2000 and was accepted most widely in 1998 (32%) (Левада- -Центр, 2009).

In 2016 we received another portion of information which was discussed in the media. Levada Center revealed that the popularity of the nationalist slogan did not change significantly. Answering the question about the attitude to this imperative, 14% of respondents declared full support, 38% were more accurate and said that such a thesis would be a good idea to implement in reasonable limits. 21% of the respondents reacted sharply to the idea saying that this was real fascism. The same percentage of the respondents answered that they were not interested in the topic. Sociologists asked people whether they should restrict the residence in the territory of Russia to representatives of certain nationalities. 20% of the respondents said that no restrictions should be introduced, 34% advocated limiting residence in Russia to people from the Caucasus, 29% were against the incomers from the former Central Asian republics of the USSR, 24% were negative towards the Chinese, 21% – to the Roma Gypsies, 19% did not want to see the Vietnamese in the Russian Federation, 13% – the Ukrainians, 6% – Jews (ZNAK, 2016; another study on the topic: Dubas, 2008, pp. 29–30).

Discussing the results presented above one has to remember that 52 per cent of the entire or relative support seems good for the nationalists for at least two reasons. Firstly, it is more than likely that in the territories which are traditionally settled by other nationalities, such as Chechnya, Buryatia or Tuva, Russian nationalistic slogans cannot be widely accepted. In other words, in the Russian ethnic territories such imperatives gain even stronger support. Secondly, the decreasing percentage of ethnic Russians in Russia leads to the tide of xenophobia. On the other hand, a strong feeling of an emerging demographic disaster in the sense of the ethnic composition of the population may lead to other acts of social unrest.

The readiness for radical action was proven in a series of violent events, especially the ones in Kondopoga, Karelia in 2006 and on Manezh square in Moscow in 2010. In Kondopoga, after a Chechen group killed two local Russians, crowds of people tried to take revenge and in fact forced many Chechens to leave the town. In Moscow the violent reaction was a result of the death of a Spartak soccer fan who was killed by five Dagestanis. During the riots 32 people were injured and, what makes the case more interesting, three members of the Other Russia: Igor Berezyuk, Ruslan Khubaev and Kirill Unchuk, were arrested, tried and sentenced to imprisonment (8, 4.5, and 3 years respectively) (Правозащитный центр "Мемориал", 2014). The probability of such phenomena to occur in the future cannot be easily estimated. However, this potential should not be entirely neglected because the trials after the Manezh events did not stop the tension (e.g. in October 2013 in Biryulovo, a district of Moscow, a huge crowd of local people attacked the properties of immigrants after the murder of a young Russian, Yegor Shcherbakov).

Concluding remarks

A critical review of the four constituting aspects leads to ambiguous conclusions about the perspectives of a national revolution in Russia.

First of all, it must be said that the first pillar of a possible revolution, the theoretical grounds, are relatively well-developed and logically structured. Russian nationalists have a lot of historical and new models of a nationalist political change at their disposal. The older models, however, seem less effective in the context of the situation in which the Russian nation is nowadays. The religious and ideological conflict with the West or another external enemy is far behind the other challenges such as the growing presence of Caucasian and Central Asian incomers, who may become the successors of ethnic Russians in the great state if the present demographic tendencies are to continue.

The analysis supports the opinion that the contemporary nationalism is conceptually divergent. One of its poles consists in Russian imperialism, political inclusivism and expansionism (deeply rooted in the previous periods of Russian history), and is generally supported by the Kremlin. The other trend – the ethnic and "exclusive" nationalism, is contested by the present elite, which perceives it as a threat to the state's integrity.

The organizational potential of Russian nationalists cannot be neglected but is generally a disputable issue. The imperialist nationalists are represented in solid structures such as the Congress of Russian Communities or the Liberal-Democratic Party of Russia. However, they are strongly subordinated to the Kremlin camp and would not gain sufficient support without the help of the government. On the other hand, the ethnically and culturally-oriented nationalists are dispersed in customarily small and suppressed organizations with no coordinative center.

The political and legal conditions for a nationalist revolution are not favorable. The non-conformists have to take into account significant problems with registration, official bans and difficulties with gaining access to the media. According to the 2002 Federal Law *On Combating Extremist Activity* several radical groups or relatively moderate organizations were erased from the official political life in Russia and no liberalization in this area can be expected.

The question about the readiness of the Russian people to support a nationalist political change in the future remains open. However, series of events such as the ones in Kondopoga in 2006 or in the very center of Moscow in 2010 provide evidence that awareness of the problem is hidden somewhere in the Russian souls and that the sleeping bear can wake up if the situation gets out of control. On the one hand, the feeling that the inner immigrants are getting a competitive advantage seems to be growing because of the objective demographic processes. On the other – the growing share of non-Russian inhabitants of the Federation may weaken the revolutionary potential.

* * *

In the 2010s, after the marginalization of oligarchs and liberal parties such as the Union of Right Forces (Союз правых сил) or the Yabloko Party (Партия "Яблоко"), Alexei Navalny, the founder of Anti-Corruption Foundation and the leader of the Progress Party, became the most recognizable symbol of Russian opposition. His political image was associated with his actions against corruption on the one hand and with the emphasis put on the interests of the Russian nation, especially in the context of the Caucasian threat, on the other. His views are perceived as "national democratic". That is why Navalny ought to be described as a representative of "vitalistic" nationalism; he generally promotes a vision of an uncorrupted state to build a healthy market economy, which brings him closer to the liberals. However, he was also strikingly critical about the Caucasian elites: both the ones connected with the Kremlin and the Islamic traditionalists or fundamentalists. Laruelle (2014) correctly points to the fact that in the activities of Navalny nationalism and liberalism are in a way reconciled.

There is a widespread opinion that Navalny is not a really strong personality but rather an artificial creation: his blog and other texts on the internet were supposed to have been produced by a team with the leader being only a supposititious figure. This might be, however, a secondary problem. What is much more important is the fact that Navalny's popularity (which became clear during the election to Moscow's City Hall), no matter what kind of personality the politician really presented, revealed a genuine need for a seemingly odd combination: Russia's rapprochement to the Euro-Atlantic civilizational standards in order to build a state which the Russian nation could ultimately treat as its own. The "restless" perception of the difficult political reality in Russia, in which Navalny is only a personification of contestation seems to be more and more congruent with Andrei Savelyev's opinion that for those who think about the salvation of the Russian nation the evolutionary option is theoretically possible but in fact not accessible because of the lack of time (Савельев, 2005).

Rewolucja, której nie było: potencjał odrodzenia rosyjskiego nacjonalizmu

W rozdziale omówiono perspektywy rewolucji nacjonalistycznej w Rosji. Badaniu poddano teoretyczną bazę, obiektywne okoliczności mogące się przyczynić do ewentualnej zmiany, potencjał organizacyjny organizacji nacjonalistycznych, warunki polityczne i nastroje rosyjskiej części obywateli Federacji Rosyjskiej.

Pierwszy filar ewentualnej rewolucji to jej fundamenty teoretyczne, stosunkowo dobrze rozwinięte i logicznie zorganizowane. Rosyjscy nacjonaliści mają do dyspozycji wiele historycznych i współczesnych modeli nacjonalistycznych przemian politycznych. Jednak starsze modele wydają się mniej skuteczne w kontekście obecnej sytuacji narodu rosyjskiego. Religijne i ideologiczne konflikty z Zachodem czy innym wrogiem zewnętrznym schodzą na dalszy plan wobec takich problemów jak rosnąca obecność kaukaskich i środkowoazjatyckich emigrantów, którzy mogą stać się następcami etnicznych Rosjan w państwie.

Analiza potwierdza pogląd, że współczesny nacjonalizm jest konceptualnie rozbieżny. Jednym z jego biegunów jest rosyjski imperializm, inkluzywność i ekspansja polityczna (głęboko zakorzenione w poprzednim okresie historii Rosji), generalnie wspierane przez Kreml. Druga tendencja – etniczny i „unikalny" nacjonalizm, poddawany krytyce przez obecną elitę, która postrzega go jako zagrożenie dla integralności państwa.

Nie należy nie doceniać organizacyjnego potencjału rosyjskich nacjonalistów, charakterystyczne są tu jednak rozproszenie i brak woli zjednoczenia. Imperialistyczni nacjonaliści reprezentowani są w tak potężnych strukturach jak Kongres Wspólnot Rosyjskich czy Polityczna Partia LDPR (wcześniej Liberalno-Demokratyczna Partia Rosji). Są silnie podporządkowani Kremlowi i nie mogą odnieść sukcesu bez pomocy rządu. Natomiast etnicznie i kulturowo zorientowani nacjonaliści są rozproszeni w różnych organizacjach, pozbawieni koordynującego centrum i są prześladowani.

Polityczne i prawne warunki dla przeprowadzenia nacjonalistycznej rewolucji nie są korzystne. Należy wziąć pod uwagę duże problemy z rejestracją, oficjalnymi zakazami, trudnościami z dostępem do mediów. Na mocy federalnej ustawy z dnia 25 lipca 2002 r. N 114-ФЗ „O przeciwdziałaniu działalności ekstremistycznej" kilka radykalnych grup bądź relatywnie umiarkowanych organizacji zostało usuniętych z oficjalnego życia politycznego w Rosji i nie przewiduje się liberalizacji w tej dziedzinie.

Kwestia gotowości Rosjan do wspierania nacjonalistycznych zmian politycznych w przyszłości pozostaje otwarta. Niemniej jednak wiele wydarzeń, takich jak zamieszki w Kondopodze w 2006 r. czy na placu Manieżnym w grudniu 2010 r., pokazuje, że świadomość problemu kryje się gdzieś w rosyjskich duszach i że śpiący niedźwiedź może się obudzić, jeśli sytuacja wymknie się spod kontroli. Z jednej strony poczucie, że wewnętrzni imigranci są bardziej konkurencyjni, wydaje się wzrastać z powodu obiektywnych procesów demograficznych. Z drugiej – udział nierosyjskich mieszkańców Federacji może osłabić potencjał rewolucyjny.

Революция, которая не произошла: потенциал возрождения русского национализма

Глава рассматривает перспективы национальной революции в России. Предметом изучения является: теоретическая база, объективные обстоятельства, способствующие возможной перемене, организационный потенциал националистских организаций, политические условия и настроения русской части населения Российской Федерации.

Первое условие возможной революции, теоретические ее основания, относительно хорошо развиты и логически структурированы. У русских националистов в распоряжении есть много «исторических» и новых моделей националистических политических перемен. Однако, более старые модели кажутся менее эффективными в контексте актуальной ситуации российской нации. Религиозно-идеологический конфликт с Западом или другим внешним врагом отходит на второй план перед такой проблемой как растущее присутствие кавказских и среднеазиатских инородцев, которые могут стать преемниками этнических русских в большом государстве.

Анализ подтверждает мнение о том, что современный национализм концептуально расходится. Одним из его полюсов является российский империализм, политическая инклюзивность и экспансионизм (глубоко укорененный в предыдущих периодах русской истории) и в целом поддерживается Кремлем. Другая тенденция – этнический и «исключительный» национализм оспаривается нынешней элитой, которая воспринимает его как угрозу целостности государства.

Организационным потенциалом русских националистов нельзя пренебрегать, однако, он подвергается дисперсии и характеризуется отсутствием воли объединения. Империалистические националисты представлены в таких мощных структурах, как Конгресс русских общин или Либерально-демократическая партия России. Они сильно подчинены кремлевскому лагерю и не в состоянии добиться успеха без помощи правительства. С другой стороны, этнически и культурно ориентированные националисты разбросаны в разных организациях, лишены единого координационного центра, и подвергаются гонениям.

Политические и правовые условия для националистической революции не благоприятны. Нонконформисты должны считаться со значительными проблемами: с регистрацией, официальными запретами, трудностями с доступом к средствам массовой информации. Согласно Федеральному Закону от 25 июля 2002 г. N 114-ФЗ «О противодействии экстремистской деятельности» несколько радикальных групп или относительно умеренных организаций были устранены из официальной политической жизни в России и никакой либерализации в этой области не ожидается.

Вопрос о готовности русского народа поддержать националистические политические изменения в будущем остается открытым. Тем не менее, ряд событий, таких как беспорядки в Кондопоге в 2006 году или на Манежной в декабре 2010 г., свидетельствует о том, что осознание проблемы скрывается где-то в российских душах и что спящий медведь может проснуться, если ситуация выйдет из-под контроля. С одной стороны, ощущение, что внутренние иммигранты получают конкурентное преимущество, похоже, растет из-за объективных демографических процессов. С другой – растущая доля нерусских жителей Федерации может ослабить революционный потенциал.

DOI: 10.12797/9788376389042.06

Joanna Rak https://orcid.org/0000-0002-0505-3684
Adam Mickiewicz University, Poznań

Chapter 5

Justifying the Use of Violence: A Gnostic Deconstruction of a Political Universe[1]

Introduction and State of the Art

The current analyses of the Russian Revolution of 1917 show that it was a by-product of successful modernization (Mironov, 2015, p. 79; Bassin, et al., 2017, p. 2). Theoretical frameworks employed to study the contentious politics draw upon the theories of anomie, disorganization, and tension. In introducing a variety of social and political factors that influenced the revolution, they concentrate on the change of living conditions, rules of behavior, social norms, anomie, attenuation of the mechanisms of social control over the individual by social organizations, disorganization

---

1 This paper is a result of the research project "Contemporary Russia: Between Authoritarianism and Totalitarianism" funded by National Science Centre, Poland. The research grant number: 2015/19/B/HS5/02516.

of society, tensions between people's needs and actual possibilities of satisfying those needs, relative deprivations, social, economic, and political grievances (Sargeant, 1997; Badcock, 2008; Mironov, 2015, p. 89). The works claim that disorientation, dysregulation, disorganization, and the intensification of tensions increased the level of deviant and protest behavior (Mironov, 2015, p. 89; Rendle and Retish, 2017). Although the existing body of work plausibly identifies the structural factors that contributed to the Russian Revolution of 1917, it understudies how political subjects triggered off their revolutionary potential (Kumar, 2015). In other words, the substantive literature avoids scrutinizing Russian political consciousness shaped by the structural factors, perpetuated, distributed and redistributed over time (Rendle, 2005; Cracraft, 2010; Michael-Matsas 2016; Rendle and Lively, 2017). Political consciousness is relatively persistent and remains after the disappearance of beings, phenomena, and processes which molded it (Wood, 2003; O'Kane, 2015). As such, it is of exploratory and explanatory power for identifying the sources and consciousness heritage of the revolution (Hickey, 2011; Beyrau, 2015).

Researchers point out that a gnosis is a form of historically--effected political consciousness characteristic of the processes of modernization, and it arises from a lust for power (Voegelin, 1997, p. 71; Hotam, 2007; Smith, 2014; Chase, 2015). The article argues that a theoretical category of political gnosis may offer a powerful conceptual framework for analyzing the sources of the Russian Revolution of 1917 identifiable on the level of political communication. It may be applied to study how political consciousness evolved over the history of Russia determined by contentious politics, what consciousness factors justify the use of political violence, and how Russian revolutionary deconstructions were reflected in political consciousness after 1917.

According to Voegelin, in political gnosis, the will to redeem ancient gnosis is combined with the "metastatic expectation of apocalypse" and "faith in the possibility of bringing about the metastasis" through human action to form the complex of revolutionary consciousness. Revolutionary consciousness is "the faith in the gnostic recipes for redemption according to which humankind is to be displaced out of the structure of temporal history and into the structure of eternal history by revolutionary action" (Voegelin, 2000, p. 205).

A classic meaning of ancient gnosis, its secularization through politicization, and criticism of modernism inform Voegelin's understanding of political gnosis. Gnosis was first defined as "knowledge" – a pure translation of the Greek *gnôsis*. However, in late antiquity, that knowledge achieved a saving role as arcane knowledge. Thereby, gnosis became a religious movement. In a narrower sense, gnosis or gnosticism is a syncretistic religious movement distributed particularly in the Eastern Mediterranean sphere of late antiquity. This movement made the elitarian "knowledge of divine secrets" the center of its theory and regarded the spiritual core of the human being as partaking in the divine substance. After having fallen into a fateful entanglement with the matter, this spiritual core can gain salvation solely through the recognition of its true, transmundane nature (Riegel, 2007, p. 214). Importantly, gnosis draws on a strict ontological dualism between the immanent, evil world of darkness and the good world of light in the beyond. As *salvator salvandus* (the savior to be saved), the saving knowledge also has a dynamic of its own: leading its immanent part to knowledge and salvation, it becomes a *salvator salvatus* (saved savior). Thus, the saving knowledge has a liberating and healing effect (Riegel, 2007, p. 214). Those features reflect Voegelin's meaning of ancient gnosis and introduce a conceptual framework of gnosis.

Since the meaning of gnosis has been changed many times to perform diverse exploratory and explanatory tasks in various scientific fields (Varshizky, 2002, p. 315), its semantic field is vague to some extent. In political sociology and philosophy, the term of gnosis occurs with a predicate of political, and the notion of political gnosis applies to describe the phenomena considered to be the sources of radical evil and the embodiment of the use of excessive political violence, such as revolution, terrorism (Pellicani, 2003), anarchism (Bamyeh, 2013, p. 192), Maoism (Grelet and Smith, 2014), Marxism, Leninism, Bolshevism (Besançon, 1981), totalitarianism (Gray, 2014), pathological sickness of political mindset, and lethal neoplasm of Western Civilization (Voegelin, 1952, p. 317; 1987, p. 112; Jonas, 1952). Those approaches are criticized for being value-laden (Miley, 2011, p. 34; Gerschewski, 2016). Furthermore, the works do not introduce the differences between gnostic and non-gnostic political consciousness. They also omit to provide us with operationalisable definitions and conceptual frameworks.

The literature review raises two research problems. First, how to categorize the differences between gnostic and non-gnostic political consciousness? Second, how to measure political gnosis? Hence, the paper aims to create a tool for both identifying the distinction between political gnosis and diagnosis and measuring the intensity of political gnosis. It consists of eight scales formulated according to the values of the essential features of political gnosis. A value is a qualitative quantity assigned to a variable (feature). Political gnosis is the set of beliefs determining the interpretation of social reality. It often serves as a justification for the use of political violence (Mulholland, 2017). The very nature of an apparatus specified by the predicate of epistemic indicates that beliefs are considered to be knowledge or knowing (Dalferth, 2004, p. 194).

The features are sufficient and necessary for an epistemic apparatus to fall into the category of political gnosis. Although single features or their values may be characteristic of other epistemic apparatuses, their configuration implies political gnosis. They are: splitting the universe of material things into the good internal world and the evil external world, dividing people into "we-insiders" and "they-outsiders", fallacious immanentization of the eschaton, self-construction of the expansionary savior to be saved, political obscurantism as a mode of dealing with dangerous knowledge, creation of the total enemy, manifestations of presumed anomie among a populace, and strategies of survival on the historic battlefield. Each feature takes on values that contribute to the extent of the intensity of political gnosis. In turn, an epistemic apparatus is non-gnostic when it does not meet the criteria for political gnosis and satisfies those for political diagnosis.

Feature № 1: The Good Internal World and the Evil External World

The first essential feature of political gnosis is a distinction between the good internal world and the evil external world, including their political values (e.g. Russia and the rest of the world). It concentrates solely on inanimate elements of the existing political reality. The distinction is a result of the semantic creation of either intrinsically good or evil worlds. It may take a form of five basic strategies that are based on the mythical structures of the images of things (Rak, 2017). On the level of the distinction between the worlds, two homogeneous criteria for the positive valorization of the internal world and the negative valorization of the external world allow us to distinguish the levels of the intensity of political gnosis. The scale ranges from (5) to (1). When a verbal expression concerning the internal and external worlds is free from attributing either positive or negative value to political reality, a feature takes on [0].

The description of the features marks the range of political gnosis determined by the level of its intensity with round brackets. Numbers in the brackets imply places on the continua. For the sake of clarity, a political diagnosis is marked with square brackets. Sufficient and necessary defining features of political gnosis and diagnosis mark out a boundary between the categories.

The distinction between the good internal and evil external worlds (f_1) takes on the following values:

(5) sacralization of the good internal world and devilization of the evil external world,

(4) hierophanization of the good internal world and demonization of the evil external world,

(3) nympholeptic melioration of the good internal world and nympholeptic pejorativization of the evil external world,

(2) counter-iconoclastic purification of the good internal world and counter-idolatric purification of the evil external world,

(1) defensive relativization of the good internal world and offensive relativization of the evil external world,

[0] political diagnosis of political reality.

The maximum extent of political gnosis (5) is when the gnostic sanctifies the internal world so much that it becomes the sacred, the greatest thing in the universe. An antinomic semantic creation focuses on the external world. The gnostic damns it so much that it is an extremely infernal evil. Adjectives in the superlative degree used to create words in that way indicate a maximum intensity of gnosis. The very high level of intensity (4) is when the internal world achieves a status of hierophany. It is a manifestation of the sacred but not the sacred itself. Although the gnostic avoids sanctifying the internal world, he or she sees it as a revelation of something greater. In contrast to hierophany, in demonization, the gnostic presents the external world as possessed. According to the narration, a demon evinces itself in the external world. The world is not the devil's spawn, but evil manifests itself in its form. Adjectives in the comparative degree serve as a means of verbal construction. The high intensity (3) is when the gnostic settles for nympholeptic creations of the worlds. Adjectives are in a positive form. They show affectionate and frenetic allegiance to the worlds under valorizing, either positive or negative. The gnostic designs the worlds by exalted manifestations of worship or aversion respectively. In the moderate intensity (2), counter--iconoclastic purification of the internal world is founded on the reduction of the diagnosed negative features of the world. The gnostic avoids making an avowal of his or her observation because he or she opposes the devaluation of the world and the decline of its positive image. The image is purified from even potentially negative qualities. Then, counter-idolatric purification of the external world is based on the reduction of the diagnosed positive features of the world. The gnostic does not disclose the discovery of its positive features. Instead, he or she rejects them actively to purify the world's image from the properties which are not bad. On the low level (1), defensive relativization depicts the elements of the good internal world as being not as evil as others. It makes use of comparisons to convince people that they are the best against the background of others. Offensive relativization of the evil external world takes advantage of the same mechanism. The gnostic presents positive components of the external world as being not as positive as others. The comparison of features serves the depreciation of that world. When a verbal expression does not take the shape of a value-laden discursive creation and is relatively close to a political diagnosis of the worlds [0], political gnosis does not emerge.

Feature № 2: "We-Insiders" and "They-Outsiders"

The second feature of political gnosis is the distinction between "we-insiders" and "they-outsiders" (e.g. Russians and non-Russians). Just like the previous feature, it consists of splitting, also called black-and-white or all-or-nothing thinking. However, in contrast to the above feature, the second one focuses on animated elements of political reality. Whereas the former concerns things and political values that constitute the gnostic's universe, the latter relates to people that are in the universe, including Paraclete who is shown and shows himself/herself as the main creator of political gnosis (e.g. he/she may be a leader of a revolution). The ontic status is a criterion for their analytical distinction, but they co-occur in the real world. The distinction is a result of a semantic creation of political subjects. It may take the form of five basic strategies that draw upon the mythical structures of the images of people (Rak, 2017). On the level of the distinction between people, two homogeneous criteria for the positive valorization of "we--insiders" and the negative valorization of "they-outsiders" enable us to distinguish four levels of the intensity of political gnosis. The scale ranges from (4) to (1). When a verbal expression concerning "we-insiders" and "they-outsiders" is free from attributing either positive or negative value to political subjects, a feature takes on [0].

The distinction between "we-insiders" and "they-outsiders" (f_2) takes on the following values:

(4) anthropolatrization of "we-insiders" and devilization of "they-insiders,"

(3) theophanization of "we-insiders" and demonization of "they--insiders,"

(2) making "we-insiders" a divine mesistes and "they-insiders" – an infernal mesistes,

(1) making "we-insiders" a katechon and "they-insiders" – an antichrist,

[0] political diagnosis of political subjects.

The maximum extent of political gnosis (4) is when the gnostic acknowledges the in-group as the divinity. The out-group is the devil incarnate. The high extent (3) is when the gnostic claims that the divinity revealed itself in the in-group. In contrast to anthropolatrization, "we-insiders" are not the god but its revelation. In demonization, a demon manifests itself in the out-group. Unlike devilization, "they-outsiders" are not a hellhound but a devil's tool. The moderate extent (2) refers to a category of a mesistes (also known as a mesidios). A mesistes is a particular type of mediator that can establish and perpetuate relations between the real and supernatural worlds thanks to his or her own unique features. A divine mesistes intercedes between a deity and people. In contrast to theophany, a mesistes is not a physical manifestation of a god, but he or she contacts a god. An infernal mesistes mediates between a devil and people not because he or she is possessed but thanks to his or her extraordinary features. The low extent (1) is when the gnostic makes "we-insiders" a katechon and "they-insiders" – an antichrist. Whereas a katechon is the one who prevents evil from destroying the world and safeguards human lives, an antichrist devastates the world and strives for its perdition. In each case, a political subject is an imagined being and may be either individual or collective. They do not have to be presented as aware of fulfilling their roles in a gnostic universe. When a verbal expression does not assume the form of a value-laden discoursive creation of an imagined subjectivity and is relatively close to a political diagnosis of political subjects [0], political gnosis does not occur.

Feature № 3: Fallacious Immanentization of the Eschaton

The analysis does not enter into a discussion on to what extent the subject matter of a discoursive creation is real and imagined, but it assumes the verbal expressions of elements of political reality as the results of a semantic creation (Shahzad, 2014). They mirror how the gnostic alters the ontological status of the existing reality by destroying and building a new one on its smoldering ruins (Pellicani, 2003, p. 11). Thus, let us emphasize that political gnosis hypostases imagined beings with words (e.g. a vision of Russia as a great power). The first two features of political gnosis concentrate on the semantic creation of the existing reality, the next one focuses on the design and performance of its future shape. The third feature of political gnosis is the fallacious immanentization of the eschaton which mirrors how eschatology affects politics (Voegelin, 1987, p. 117). The gnostic fallaciously immanentizes the eschaton by projecting eschatological visions for the world and implements a policy to actualize them (Voegelin, 1987, p. 166). Immanentization is fallacious because the projects of eternal salvation are of political rather than religious nature (Voegelin, 1987, p. 120). Political gnosis is gradable under a criterion of a variant of immanentization of the eschaton which provides the gnostic's life with sense. The distinction is a result of a semantic creation of what political reality should dawn and how to achieve that dreamful state. It may take the form of four basic strategies that emanate from Voegelin's variants of immanentization (Voegelin, 1987). On the level of the fallacious immanentization, a homogeneous criterion of the feasibility of the eschaton enables us to distinguish four levels of the intensity of political gnosis. The scale ranges from (4) to (1). When a verbal expression concerning the future of political reality is free from overtly dreamlike visions, a feature takes on [0].

The fallacious immanentization of the eschaton (f_3) takes on the following values:

(4) active mysticism,
(3) utopianism,
(2) eutopianism,
(1) progressivism,
[0] political diagnosis of current efforts to develop the state.

The scale is based on Voegelin's three variants of fallacious immanentization: active mysticism, utopianism, and progressivism, but it modifies the framework to enhance its methodological and expected empirical effectiveness. According to Voegelin, in active mysticism (4), a state of perfection is to be obtained through a revolutionary transfiguration of the nature of a man. Let us go a step further and add that active mysticism consists of the performance of a fully unrealistic vision of the eschaton. The gnostic declares the use of available and inaccessible means to perform the eschaton. As Voegelin argues, utopianism concentrates on the state of perfection, without clarity about the means that are required for its performance. It may assume two forms. First, it may be an axiological dream world when the gnostic is aware that the eschaton is unrealizable. Second, it may take the form of social idealism. The distinction between the forms remains unclear. Whereas the first locates just in an awareness sphere, the second is verbally expressible. Here, within the scale, utopianism (3) is when the gnostic creates a wholly unrealistic vision of the eschaton and declares the deployment of available means to actualize it. Unlike utopia, eutopia embodies a possible concept. Eutopianism (2) draws upon a realistic vision of the eschaton and making declarations of the actualization of the eschaton. The gnostic presumes the employment of available means to immanentize his or her vision. It is utopistics in Wallerstein's (1998, p. 1) understanding. As Voegelin indicates, progressivist immanentization (1) focuses on a movement towards a goal, a beatific vision that is a state of perfection. The progressivist gnostic does not provide clarity about the final perfection, but it need not be clarified because he or she takes a selection of desirable factors as the standard and interprets progress as a qualitative and quantitative rise of the present good – the "bigger and better." Unless he or she adjusts the original standard to the changing political situation, it becomes reactionary (Voegelin, 1987, pp. 120–121). It means that progressivist immanentization concentrates on the rather realistic but not well-defined eschaton. The gnostic introduces ways towards its achievement. Whereas the gnostic verbally creates a heaven on earth, the diagnostic avoids introducing his or her unrealistic expectations. When a verbal expression does not take the form of a value-laden discoursive creation and is relatively close to a political diagnosis of prospective political reality [0], political gnosis does not occur.

Feature № 4: Presumed Anomie

The fourth feature of political gnosis is presumed anomie. The gnostic that creates and distributes political gnosis assumes that its recipients feel anomie and thus he or she refers to anomie's supposititious features (e.g. a vision of relative deprivation in social security). Anomie is instability resulting from a breakdown of the regulatory order that secures norms (Braithwaite, et al., 2010, p. 17). Even though it is an opportune awareness undertow for political gnosis (Bäcker, 2011, p. 195), it also informs a semantic resource of political gnosis as a reaction to the existing populace and world condition. The gnostic seeks to distribute political gnosis effectively to win political believers over and encourage them to redistribute political gnosis. He or she makes provision for the properties of actual anomie to make his or her expressed vision of anomie the reflection of reality. His or her presuming, however, is not contingent on the actual anomie. It is just a goal--driven semantic creation which may take on a variety of values.

The scale to measure an extent of the intensity of the feature of political gnosis benefits from Heydari, Davoudi and Teymoori's set of indicators of anomie (2011). The set comprehensively, critically, and skillfully summarizes and develops current scales of anomie. The authors define three major groups of indicators: meaninglessness and distrust, powerlessness, and fetishism of money. Meaninglessness and distrust find expression in eight statements: (i) I can trust the statements of high-ranking officials (authority), (ii) There is little use in writing to public officials because they often aren't really interested in the problems of the average man, (iii) In spite of what some people say, the lot of the average man is getting worse, not better, (iv) I believe most of the congress bills are towards the welfare of people, (v) Most public officials (people in public office) are not really interested in the problems of the average man, (vi) I often wonder what the meaning of life really is, (vii) It's hardly fair to bring children into the world with the way things look for the future, (viii) Everything is relative, and there just aren't any definite rules to live by. Powerlessness expresses itself in seven statements: (i) I lead a trapped or frustrated life, (ii) Nobody knows what is expected of him or her in life, (iii) I have no control over my destiny, (iv) The socioeconomic status of people determines their dignity and it is inevitable, (v) The world is changing so fast that it is hard for me to understand what is going on, (vi) My whole world feels like it is falling apart, (vii) No matter how hard people try in life, it doesn't make any difference. Fetishism of money is expressed in five statements: (i) To make money, there are no right and wrong ways anymore, only easy ways and hard ways, (ii) A person is justified in doing almost anything if the reward is high enough, (iii) I am getting a college education so I can get a good job, (iv) I follow whatever rules I want to follow, (v) Money is the most important thing in life (Heydari, Davoudi and Teymoori, 2011, p. 1089). Verbal expressions which fall into the statement category are the elements of political gnosis called presumed anomie.

On the level of presumed anomie, two homogeneous criteria for the anomie indicators and statements enable us to distinguish three levels of the intensity of political gnosis. The scale ranges from (3) to (1). When a verbal expression concerning presumed anomie is free from the references to the statements, a feature takes on [0].

The presumed anomie (f_4) takes on the following values:

(3) three types of the anomie indicators and at least 50% of the statements of each one,

(2) two types of the anomie indicators and at least 50% of the statements of each one,

(1) one type of the anomie indicators and at least 50% of its statements,

[0] political diagnosis of relative deprivation.

The maximum extent of political gnosis (3) is when the gnostic presumes anomie that finds expression in meaninglessness and distrust, powerlessness, and fetishism of money. At least 50% of the statements of each indicator are in use. Political gnosis achieves the moderate extent (2) when the gnostic takes advantage of two out of the three indicators and at least 50% of the statements of each one. The low extent (1) occurs when the gnostic refers to one from among the three indicators and at least 50% of its defining statements. When a verbal expression does not take the shape of a value-laden discursive creation of a response to the presumed anomie and is relatively close to a political diagnosis of relative deprivation [0], political gnosis does not emerge.

Feature № 5: Total Enemy

The research avoids employing the category of the objective enemy because it is strongly associated with totalitarianism (Arendt, 1973, pp. 422–423). Instead, it defines political gnosis by the feature of the semantic creation of the total enemy (e.g. enemy of the people). Thorup defines the total enemy as the one whose identity and deeds are substituted for analogies and being; whose the only one goal in life is to destroy and deploy violence; who is present even if not apparent; whose enmity comes from a being rather than an action; and with whom coexistence is impossible due to the fact that the total enemy will never let go and allow peace and prosperity to become the order of the day (2015, p. X). The total enemy is to be found, punished, and annihilated because it impedes any immanentization of the eschaton and threatens the existence of the in-group. It is a source of great and everlasting insecurity.

On the level of the total enemy that jeopardizes gnostic enterprises, two homogeneous criteria of the expectedness of the total enemy's shape and the extent of the establishment of in-group political values under the total enemy threat enable us to distinguish four levels of the intensity of political gnosis. The scale ranges from (4) to (1). When a verbal expression concerning obstacles to development is free from the category of the total enemy, a feature takes on [0].

The creation of the total enemy in relation to in-group political values (f_5) takes on the following values:

(4) moral-nihilistic creation of the total enemy in relation to a floating set of political values,

(3) moral-nihilistic creation of the total enemy in relation to a fixed set of political values,

(2) fundamentalist creation of the total enemy in relation to a floating set of political values,

(1) fundamentalist creation of the total enemy in relation to a fixed set of political values,

[0] intersubjective political diagnosis of obstacles to the community's development.

The maximum extent of political gnosis (4) is when the gnostic employs moral nihilism to produce the total enemy. Members of a populace can never be quite sure that they will not fall into some future category of the total enemy because it may be changed and supplemented over time (Court, 2008, p. 107). The gnostic claims that the total enemy stops the immanentization of the eschaton and puts many things significant to a populace in jeopardy. It is erratic what political values, apart from the core ones, contribute to the creation of relations between the total enemy and other semantic creations. The high extent (3) is when people cannot predict who or what will become the total enemy because it is continually under construction. The total enemy undermines immanentization of the eschaton and threatens the gnostic's resources. The gnostic has, however, a rigid set of political values that are to be protected from the total enemy. Unpredictability-driven fear is a result of the most intensive types of political gnosis which make use of moral-nihilism. In turn, a firm agenda mirroring a hierarchy of political values contributes to less intense fundamentalist political gnosis by arming it with relative predictability. The moderate extent (2) occurs when the gnostic distributes a consistent vision of the total enemy. People know how to recognize it, and the criteria for recognition are invariable. Nevertheless, that well-determined total enemy puts a variety of volatile political values at risk. The low extent (1) typifies a fundamentalist project of the total enemy. The fundamentalist gnostic creates a consistent image of the total enemy. Members of a populace know the criteria for its distinction and are sure what and who meets the essential criteria to be the total enemy. That figure impedes the immanentization of the eschaton as well as the firmly established and hierarchized political values. When a verbal expression does not take the shape of a value-laden discursive creation of the total enemy that endangers gnostic enterprises and is relatively close to an intersubjective political diagnosis of obstacles to the community's development [0], political gnosis does not take place.

Feature № 6: Expansionary Savior to be Saved

According to a politico-soteriological gnostic view, the gnostic is a savior to be saved. It means that the gnostic has knowledge of how to be saved through the immanentization of the eschaton, performs eschatological goals, and saves others from extinction by sharing knowledge and immanentizing the eschaton together. At a declarative level, he or she saves himself/herself, others, and will be saved. The expansionary nature of the savior to be saved finds expression in the search for savable non-gnostics (e.g. Russian compatriots (Grigas, 2016, p. 2)). Apart from unambiguous divisions between the in-group, the out-group, the good internal world and the evil external world, the gnostic detects some group of people who may become a material resource of the internal world. They are neither part of the in-group nor belonging to the evil external world. They do not belong under the total enemy. As such, they may be saved rather than doomed to extinction like the out-group.

On the level of the expansionary savior to be saved, a homogeneous criterion of the source of non-gnostics' predisposition to become gnostics allows us to distinguish four levels of the intensity of political gnosis. The scale ranges from (4) to (1). When a verbal expression concerning external political subjects is free from overtly soteriological attempts to change their status to a political structure, a feature takes on [0].

The expansion of the savior to be saved (f_6) takes on the following values:

(4) voluntarist rescue operation,
(3) subjective rescue operation,
(2) objective rescue operation,
(1) fatalistic rescue operation,
[0] political diagnosis of external political subjects in relation to domestic and exterior political structures.

The maximum extent of political gnosis (4) occurs when the gnostic refers to the knowledge-driven will to semantically inform a rescue operation aiming at transforming non-gnostics into in--group gnostics and building them into the good internal world. The gnostic avoids introducing the perspective of the would-be material resource. The other three semantic strategies relativize the sources of the predisposition. The high extent (3) is when the gnostic refers to the passionate desire of a subject formed by non-gnostics to join in-group gnostics and become the part of the good internal world. The gnostic shows the subject as enticed into immanentizing the eschaton together and thus thirsting the future, secular and political salvation. The moderate extent (2) is if the gnostic objectifies the rescue mission by giving it objective values to introduce it as generally beneficial. The source of the operation is general knowledge rather than gnostics' or non-gnostics' will. The low extent (1) typifies a fatalistic semantic creation of the rescue operation. As the gnostic claims, there is nothing left but to save non-gnostics, and this is not a matter of anybody's choice. When a verbal expression does not take the form of a value-laden discoursive creation of the rescue operation aiming at expanding the savior to be saved and is relatively close to an intersubjective political diagnosis of external political subjects in relation to domestic and exterior political structures [0], political gnosis does not make an appearance.

Despite non-gnostics' predisposition to be saved, they must not immanentize their eschaton. Let us bring back Buckley's (2007, p. 24) famous phrase "Don't let THEM immanentize the eschaton! [original spelling – J. R.]" to delve into the very nature of the conditions of the savior's to be saved expansion. Non--gnostics must attach themselves or be taken into the in-group soteriology. Otherwise, they fall into the out-group or the total enemy category.

Feature № 7: Political Obscurantism

Obscurantism consists of purposeful withholding knowledge from members of a populace. The gnostic imposes restrictions of disseminating knowledge to prevent facts from becoming known (e.g. current economic rates in the world). Thus, he or she strives to maintain the shape of a gnostic universe under construction. On the level of political obscurantism, one homogeneous criterion of a strategy of coping with non-gnostic knowledge lets us define three levels of the intensity of political gnosis. Non--gnostic knowledge is of a dangerous nature because it potentially or genuinely precludes the immanentization of the eschaton, supports the out-group, the evil external world, the total enemy, and threatens the in-group and the good internal world. The scale ranges from (3) to (1). When a verbal expression concerning knowledge is free from attempts to stop its spread and politicize its nature, a feature takes on [0].

Political obscurantism (f_7) takes on the following values:
(3) exterminating dangerous knowledge,
(2) faking dangerous knowledge,
(1) tabooing dangerous knowledge,
[0] discussion over the diagnosed knowledge of political meaning.

The maximum extent of political gnosis (3) occurs when the gnostic displays overt hostility to dangerous knowledge which is to be destroyed due to its very nature. The moderate extent (2) is when the gnostic presents non-gnostic knowledge as fake knowledge that misleads. The low extent (1) makes an appearance when the gnostic taboos non-gnostic knowledge. Since tabooing draws upon making things unmentionable, dangerous knowledge does not enter the gnostic's statements. When a verbal expression does not take the shape of a value-laden discursive creation of the eradication of dangerous knowledge, and it is relatively close to contributing to the discussion over diagnosed knowledge of political meaning [0], political gnosis does not appear.

Feature № 8: Survival on the Historic Battlefield

Political gnosis gives temporal solutions which stem from a desire of self-perpetuation. The gnostic introduces strategies of how to survive on the historic battlefield of the clash of good and evil powers (e.g. a revolutionary situation). Unlike the features of political gnosis that depict how the in-group/out-group and the good/evil worlds look like, and in contrast to the future--oriented immanentization of the eschaton, the following feature concentrates on the strategies of coping with being here and now. On the level of the strategies of the survival on the battlefield, two homogeneous criteria for responding to non-gnostic cultural resources and treating gnostic cultural resources enable us to determine three levels of the intensity of political gnosis (Rak, 2015a; 2015b; 2016). The scale ranges from (3) to (1). When a verbal expression concerning the use of cultural resources in daily life is free from the references to the statements, a feature takes on [0].

The strategies of survival on a historic battlefield (f_8) take on the following values:
(3) annihilating contra-acculturation and celebrating nativism,
(2) isolating contra-acculturation and preserving nativism,
(1) escapist contra-acculturation and reviving nativism,
[0] political diagnosis of how to use or avoid using cultural resources.

The maximum extent of political gnosis (3) is when the gnostic claims that non-gnostic cultural resources are to be annihilated. Simultaneously, the gnostic celebrates gnostic resources by making use of its valuable potential to survive. The moderate extent (2) makes an appearance when the gnostic comes out in favor of isolation from non-gnostic cultural resources. The gnostic perpetuates his or her own cultural facilities. The low extent (1) occurs when the gnostic escapes from being in any relationship with non-gnostic cultural resources. He or she makes attempts to revive the weakened cultural base. When a verbal expression does not take the form of contra-acculturative and nativist approach towards cultural resources and is relatively close to an intersubjective political diagnosis of their use [0], political gnosis does not show up.

Conclusions

The chapter makes a methodological contribution to the growing body of literature concerning political gnosis. It creates the research tool for differentiating between political diagnosis and gnosis and measuring the intensity of the latter on the basis of the qualitative indicators. Each out of the eight defining features takes on values that contribute to the level of the intensity of political gnosis. Every time before their application to empirical research, they should be operationalized according to the character of the sources to be analyzed.

In political reality, the pure ideal types of neither political gnosis nor diagnosis occur. Instead, their features co-occur in various configurations. It means that in a political text, a researcher may find both gnosis and diagnosis even on the level of the same feature. The former may take on a variety of values which indicate its intensity. When verbal expressions of a feature are diversified in terms of intensity, a researcher has to estimate which value is dominant and what characterizes the configuration of values.

These considerations innitiate an academic debate over the measurement of political gnosis and as such avoids proposing a final conceptual framework. Instead, it brings researchers in to analyze its methodological and theoretical assumptions critically and make research attempts to contribute to the field. Researchers may develop the tool by both discussing the quality and properties of its structure and testing its empirical effectiveness. Revolutionary, non-revolutionary, pre-revolutionary and post-revolutionary thinking offer a challenging research field. It may be helpful to evaluate how well the tool performs its methodological function within an analysis. One may also wish to rethink and modify the necessary and sufficient criteria for an epistemic apparatus to fall into the categories of political gnosis and diagnosis. The already proposed scales may be extended to improve their sensitivity to the details. The more precise the scale is, the more detailed the research results are.

Usprawiedliwienie zastosowania przemocy: gnostyczna dekonstrukcja wszechświata politycznego

Celem artykułu jest stworzenie narzędzia badawczego służącego do rozróżniania gnostycznej i niegnostycznej świadomości politycznej oraz mierzenia natężenia pierwszej z wymienionych. Gnoza polityczna to aparat epistemiczny, który przybiera formę konfiguracji przekonań określających interpretację rzeczywistości społecznej. Wystarczające i konieczne cechy definiujące gnozę polityczną są następujące: podział uniwersum rzeczy materialnych na dobry świat wewnętrzny i zły świat zewnętrzny, rozróżnienie ludzi na „nas-swoich" i „ich--obcych", fałszywa immanentyzacja eschatonu, manifestacje domniemanej anomii wśród populacji, stworzenia wroga totalnego, autokreacja ekspansywnego zbawiciela, który ma zostać zbawiony, polityczny obskurantyzm jako sposób radzenia sobie z niebezpieczną wiedzą i strategie przetrwania na historycznym polu bitwy. Każda cecha przybiera wartości, które wskazują poziom natężenia gnozy politycznej. Wkładem opracowania do metodologii socjologii polityki jest zestaw wskaźników i skali pozwalający badaczowi identyfikować i porównywać werbalne wyrazy gnozy politycznej. Co więcej, rozwija ono metodologię badania gnozy politycznej za sprawą kryteriów rozróżnienia politycznej diagnozy od gnozy.

Оправдание насилия: гностическая деконструкция политической вселенной

Цель этой главы – создать исследовательский инструмент для измерения интенсивности и определения различий между гностическим и негностическим политическим сознанием. Политический гнозис – это эпистемический аппарат, который принимает форму конфигурации убеждений, определяющих интерпретацию социальной реальности. Достаточные и необходимые черты, определяющие политический гнозис следующее: разделение вселенной материальных вещей на хороший внутренний мир и плохой внешний мир, разделение людей на «нас-своих» и «их-чужих», ложная имманентизация эсхатона, проявления предполагаемой аномии среди населения, создание тотального врага, создание экспансивного спасителя, который должен быть спасен, политический обскурантизм, как способ справиться с опасными знаниями, а также стратегии выживания на поле битвы истории. Каждая черта принимает ценности, указывающие интенсивность политического гнозиса. Вклад настоящего исследования в методологию социологии политики это предоставление набора показателей и шкал, позволяющих исследователю определять и сравнивать словесные выражения политического гнозиса. Более того, оно разрабатывает методологию изучения политического гнозиса по критериям различения политического диагноза и гнозиса.

DOI: 10.12797/9788376389042.07

JOACHIM DIEC ⓘD https://orcid.org/0000-0002-3335-3772

Conclusions
The Deconstructive Power of the Russian Revolution

The time that has passed since the beginning of the Russian Revolution is long enough to work out some interpretative formulas of its consequences. In the 19th century, in his treaties about the Western world and Russia, the Russian poet and political thinker Fyodor Tyutchev (1803–1873) described the latter as the embodiment of an eternal providential empire whose mission is continually distorted by a diabolic power – the Revolution (Тютчев, 2013). As it turned out after a couple of decades, it was just Russia that became both the victim and the den of evil: the Revolution of 1917 took a specifically Russian shape even though it originally refuted the national idea.

In the course of time, the state that had grown on the revolutionary soil changed its image several times. According to Chaadaev's generalizations, which were mentioned in the introduction, Russia is abnormally vulnerable to radical transformations. This does not necessarily refer only to the great shifts of paradigms such as the Petrine reforms or the collapse of the old empire and the establishment of a communist state. Even within the Soviet period, everyday life and institutions looked significantly different in 1924, 1938, 1957 or in the 1970s. Dmitry Trenin realizes that in the very beginning the Russian Revolution was permeated by universalistic messianism. However, in the mid-1920s the paradigm of the Soviet state turned into a fortress mentality: the USSR was the only genuinely socialist country in the world (as it was in the case of the only Orthodox state – the Third Rome – in the 16th century) surrounded by capitalist powers. After WW2, we dealt with "the socialist camp", and after 1960 – with "the socialist community" which fought against the "world imperialism" with the United States at the helm. This competition led to longitudinal tension and to the collapse of the USSR in the end (Тренин, 2012, pp. 274–275).

Trying to answer the questions which were declared as the leitmotif of our study, we can initially point to the conclusion that the ideas, actions and consequences of the revolution result from a certain kind of unnaturalness. Its base is formed by the belief in the necessity of legal supremacy of ideas, such as the happiness of the people or the glory of a state or nation, over everyday needs and individual ambitions. The revolution originally fulfilled the dreams of several generations of Russian Marxists and Populists (*Narodniki, Народники*), who preached about the oppression which was experienced by the Russian people, especially peasants and workers. However, the new system managed to rob them of any individual property and individual rights. The life and dreams of the individual turned out to be trivial in the clash with the "just cause": a peasant who, just before WW1, was ultimately liberated from control and became the owner of his plot of land had to first face the duty of compulsory deliveries after 1917 and then, after 1928, the tragedy of collectivization.

Another source of unnaturalness lies in the conviction that the state (or any other collective organization) has a universal or divine mission. The pattern of such thinking comes from great religions, e.g. Shinto, Zoroastrianism, Judaism, Christianity or Islam. These missions, however, are generally oriented toward transcendental reality even if they concern human behavior and preoccupations. In the case of the Russian Revolution, contrary to most of the previous ones, it is a deterministic, post-Hegelian scheme that underlay the revolutionary actions and lawmaking. The assumption that the state might play an important part in the divine plan is close to the idea of the Byzantine diarchy or the Islamic caliphate, so one can seek some earlier patterns. Nevertheless, all of them treat the supernatural world as the main point of reference. In the case of the Marxist Revolution, the ultimate cause lies in the earthly state itself.

Such an attitude is linked to the idea that the essence of the mission can be expressed and successfully realized in laws and political actions. Law in the revolutionary perspective was treated neither as a set of practical regulations that can make the functioning of the state and society safer and more effective nor as a realization of a higher order. There was a lot of criticism of law in Russia under the old regime: it was usually accused of overregulation and allegiance to conservative values. However, the legal framework of the empire made it ineffective only in some way, whereas the Soviet law created a totally dysfunctional state, which finally collapsed after 70 years of totalitarian management. After the revolution, several legal solutions, as we can read in the first chapter, still influence today's Russian legislation, especially in the area of business and the relation of citizens with foreign legal and natural persons.

The essential place of law in the structure of Russia's dysfunctionality cannot be neglected. As a number of researchers have noted, law in Russia is perceived not as a core social value but as an instrument for the leaders. In the long history of the country, law was often criticized as a barrier to efficient policies. It is the central authority that is equipped with common trust and a providential mission. The same can be said about the advantage of politics over the economy. It is the central power that has always decided about the shape of economic relations. The situation is not very different in today's capitalist Russia, where all basic flows are controlled by the administration (Bieleń, 2014, pp. 211–212).

The unnaturalness of the main convictions in revolutionary thinking also stems from the belief that human needs are permanent and that there is an intelligible way in which we could meet them. The Russian Empire was authoritarian, not totalitarian, requiring obedience but not necessarily spiritual devotion (contrary to Pre-Petrine Moscovia). Some of the populist and revolutionary socialists, especially Petr Tkachov, postulated the standardization of needs and the physical liquidation of the older generation, which was supposed to be incapable of building a brave new and totally structuralized society. This kind of thinking was taken over by the Bolsheviks who created a political, economic and social system which lacked mental diversity. The system was uniform under the vertical leadership of the party, the economy was a leading example of inefficient central planning. In the area of culture and education, for a long time only the correct ideological (Marxist) and artistic (socialist realistic) lines were accepted. However, what seems paradoxical, it is the non-conformist activity that contributed to relative success in the USSR: the space breakthroughs, sport achievements or famous pieces in the movie industry or literature with Pasternak and Solzhenitsyn.

The second essential problem of the following study lies in the issue of *equality*: the problem of *the people* and of *the elite*. Whereas natural order (at least in the Hoppean explication) assumes a spontaneous emergence of *nobilitas naturalis*, the Bolshevik doctrine imposes different solutions. First of all, it aims at the creation of an entirely egalitarian society. This vision is by all means utopian but many studies on totalitarian utopias describe and cleverly generalize such phenomena. The Bolshevik dream neglects natural differences probably not only because it is a utopian idea. The attempt, which was doomed to fail from the very beginning, was in fact a powerful step toward the eradication of these disproportions. It was a dramatic struggle of those who were highly dissatisfied with the shape of the real world in which they were born: in the wrong country or ethnic group, in the wrong place or social class.

Measures were undertaken to even the social and economic status of Russian citizens: people of the lowest classes became officers and state officials, representatives of the nobility and bourgeoisie were expelled and even food was rationed at the very beginning of the Bolshevik era (according to the regulations of war communism). However, after a decade it turned out that there were some citizens who were more equal than others. Since the 1930s, the Stalinist regime consisted not only in the totalitarian dictatorship of one person but also in the power of the secret police, which had enormous prerogatives. Then, in the 1960s and 1970s the *nomenklatura*, a certain new class of well-established party officials, began to dominate in spite of the egalitarian ideology (Đilas, 1957). Even in the circumstances of such an ideological atmosphere, the system appeared incapable of any successful struggle against natural processes of the circulation of elites.

After the collapse of the red empire, in the 1990s, the Family (the people closest to President Boris Yeltsyn) and the oligarchs became the new elite of the "robbed country". Since 2000, the Putin team of secret service and military officials have established their supremacy in the name of the struggle against the old and bad oligarchy within the country and against the Western domination in international relations. In none of the cases has the Russian political system helped to work out a *nobilitas naturalis* that would be allowed to develop the country in an unrestricted way. The old oligarchs gained their property because of their connections with those who controlled the financial flows and decided about the economic shape of the country. However, they generally took advantage of their own smartness and initiative. The new elite predominantly used violence and restrictions subordinating the

Russian economy to the expectations of statists but the level of inequality within the country became even more appalling.

This, in the end, makes us inquire about the relation between the *revolution* and the *natural order*. The notion of *natural order* includes several disputable aspects. First of all, it does not refer directly to the *state of nature*. Contrary to that, it combines two tendencies. On the one hand, it is based on realism concerning the laws of nature, i.e. human corporeality. On the other – it tries to meet something actually absent in nature: the need for harmonious development in the material and mental spheres. For some it might be the never ending search for the undefinable *dào* (道); for others – a quest for a life formed according to the biblical commandments and reflections: "fill the earth and subdue it" (Genesis, 1, 28), "For my thoughts are not your thoughts, neither are your ways my ways (Isaiah, 55, 8–9)" and St. Augustine's famous conviction that "You have made us for yourself, O Lord, and our heart is restless until it rests in you" (Augustine, *Confessions*, Lib. 1,1–2,2.5,5; CSEL 33, 1–5).

Such a concept is by no means abstract. Contrary to many "realistic" theories, it leads the analyst to the study of real processes in which one focuses on the technological, economic and social development of nations. There is no such thing as unlimited development in the *state of nature* but it can be considered if one refers to *natural order*. It is possible to describe the demographic dynamics, which seems to be relatively positive from the perspective of the whole of mankind but not necessarily in the case of Russia and the West. It is not difficult to estimate life expectancy, infant mortality, the length of time a citizen must be employed to afford one square foot of real estate or the participation in NCO. Even the level of happiness becomes an object of sociological research (Левада-Центр, 2014). In other words, it is relatively possible to estimate to what extent a state or a certain system meets the expectations of *regular* and, what is no less important, *unrestricted* development of the citizens, so that they continually get healthier and happier but also increasingly motivated to reach the next stages of health, satisfaction, wealth and happiness.

There is no doubt that such categories (as mentioned above) can be expressed only by means of indirect statistical indicators. However, if compared to the revolutionary imperatives such as *equality, brotherhood* or *social justice*, they still seem quite scientific.

If one looks critically at the categories of *natural order* and those of *the revolution*, it is possible to discern a specific relation between them since the revolutionary thinking is by no means autonomous; it is a dark shadow of the natural search for goodness. Let us have a look at the basic oppositions which are relevant to the natural order paradigm and the new proposal promoted by Bolshevism. For a reasonable simplification, we will use the term "traditional" for the categories of the *natural order* paradigm and the adjective "revolutionary" to express the ones that underlie the revolutionary thinking.

1. The traditional opposition of **prosperity** versus **poverty** was replaced by the revolutionary one of **social justice** versus **social injustice**.
2. The traditional opposition of **God-given individual freedom** versus **slavery (created by imperfect man)** was replaced by the revolutionary one of **freedom as consciousness of necessity** versus **class unconsciousness**.
3. The traditional opposition of **political liberty – totalitarianism** was replaced by the revolutionary one of **liberation of the proletariat** versus **social oppression**.
4. The traditional opposition of **human dignity – degradation (animalization)** was replaced by the revolutionary one of **communist relations of production** versus **historically backward relations of production**. The individual dignity for the Bolsheviks was only a product of the superstructure (comp. Bochenski, 1963, pp. 119–120).

5. The traditional opposition of **legal equality** versus **legal inequality** was replaced by the revolutionary one of **equality in the access to goods** versus **inequality in the access to goods**.

6. The traditional opposition of **respect for property** versus **theft** was replaced by the revolutionary one of **liberation from private property** versus *kulak* **mentality**.

7. The traditional opposition of **respect for individual life and health** versus **murder/disrespect for health** was replaced by the revolutionary one of **respect for the "collective man"** (individual lives were obviously unimportant) versus **disrespect for the interests of the proletariat** (Fülöp-Miller, 1965, pp. 7–8).

8. The traditional opposition of **solidarity** versus **discord** was replaced by the revolutionary one of **class consciousness** (comp. Goldman, 1971, pp. 69–70) versus **class treason**.

9. The traditional opposition of **competition for perfection** versus destructive **uniformity** was replaced by the revolutionary one of **collective work (Stakhanov ethic)** versus **sabotage**.

10. The traditional opposition of **equal opportunities** versus **unequal opportunities** was replaced by the revolutionary one of the **satisfaction of needs** vs **failure to satisfy needs** (according to the belief that "all stomachs are created equal").

11. The traditional opposition of **highest harmony** versus **chaos** was replaced by the revolutionary one of **classless society** versus **class struggle**.

12. Last but not least, the traditional opposition of *nobilitas naturalis* versus *populus naturalis* was replaced by the revolutionary one of **the avant-garde of the proletariat (the Party)** versus **the Proletariat** itself (the not entirely self-conscious subject of historical development).

As observed in Toynbee's *Study of History*, after some time the *creative minority* inevitably turns into the *dominant minority* (Toynbee, 1939, pp. 35ff, 445ff, 459ff). However, the natural elite is not a closed and established class. It is rather a constantly changing group where some people are continually replaced by others as a result of the functioning market. The avant-garde of the proletariat is a different story: the party members become state officials and are able to establish laws that protect them from natural competition (Đilas, 1957).

This short overview opens the door to generalization: one may realize that the new revolutionary oppositions can be described as *deconstructed* forms of the traditional ones. We decided to categorize the revolutionary paradigm in such a way because the Russian Revolution turned against many more values than the ones represented by the old regime. The Bolsheviks and other radical revolutionaries tried to demolish any inequality without reflection about the natural character of the emergence of elites and avoided considerations about the temporariness and randomness of injustice in their own lives and in the whole Russian Empire.

Finally, there is an obvious need for a glimpse into the relation between the Russian Revolution and natural order in the pragmatic perspective. An objective and just evaluation of the revolution and the following Soviet period in Russian history is hardly possible. As stated in the second chapter of our book, Russia still looks at itself through the prism of its Soviet past and is by all means under the impression of the trauma that arose after the collapse of the red empire.

In many bitter ways, the Russia of the 21st century is still a shadow of its previous greatness both in the material and moral dimensions. According to Maxim Kalashnikov, who resorts to Victor I. Petrik's sociological research, the Post-Soviet anthropological type is much more passive than its Soviet predecessor. Today's Russia has become a state where the leading role both in ideology and economy belongs to "ruminants" (жвачные) – people who do not believe that a technological breakthrough is possible in their country: everything important has already been invented and even if there is a chance of some new ideas, they will appear in the West rather than in Russia (Калашников, 2014, p. 188).

This nostalgic tone, however, seems to be justified only if one compares the Soviet times with the period of the Russian Federation. A comparison of the economic dynamics of the Russian Empire in the last decades of its existence with analogous data concerning the USSR leaves no doubt. No one could neglect the obvious achievements in education, science or health care in the Soviet Union. Nevertheless, it is essential to remember that GDP per capita, if related to the level of more advanced countries, fell from 28% – 30% in 1913 to 16 – 18% in 1990 (Meliantsev, 2004, pp. 106, 120). In other words, the balance of the old times was more impressive.

The problem obviously lies not only in the disputable achievements in the country's economy. Under the early Bolshevik regime and in the USSR, the inhabitants of the huge territory experienced unprecedented terror. There are various estimates as to the number of victims in the Soviet Union. Hosking (2001, p. 469) supposes that only in the 1930s the death toll reached about 10-11 million. If one takes into account the victims of the Red Terror, the unnecessary casualties during WW2 and the prisoners of the Gulag, we are left with the image of a demographic disaster. Ruined health, broken personalities, and a slave mentality of the *Homo Sovieticus* are the next signs of destruction that became the daily bread of millions.

Can the successor of the USSR be treated as a country that rejected all Soviet curses? It seems that pessimistic opinions prevail among average Russians. A clever explanation of the economic and civilizational failure was provided by Andrei Piontkovsky, who makes a distinction between the economic reforms in Russia and Central Europe. In the latter, privatization was clearly "unjust" since many of the previous managers came into property that had never been theirs in the legal sense. However, they took care of it anyway and were able to act in the circumstances of the free market. This led to natural competition, where the "unrighteous" brainy leaders pushed the less efficient ones out of the market. The same was expected in Russia but the result was different. The "principle of injustice" was not limited to the moment of original distribution but was continued in the next two decades. The new formation is continually mutating, remaining neither capitalist nor socialist. The oligarchs became mandarins rather than business people and managed to rob Russia of enormous wealth, which then appeared on their accounts beyond the borders of the Eurasian Economic Union (Пионтковский, 2011, p. 392).

The Russian Revolution not only became a tragically consistent attempt to realize a utopian gnostic vision, based on radical oppositions, but also a far-reaching process in which, willingly or not, the new distinctions appeared to be a deconstructed version of those which are dictated by the logic of Natural Order. In this sense the legacy of the Russian Revolution is a gigantic lie, a false mirror which still torments the citizens in the largest part of the post-Soviet area: the official rhetoric remains populist but the state – strictly oligarchic. The idea of international diversity and multipolarity is a hidden concept of leaving a great number of nations without security and the rejection of today's internal and international leadership is only a hidden and selfish form of promoting another order of much more severe inequality. The idea of brotherhood justifies the invasion of brothers. The declared necessity of strength is in fact a desperate attempt to regain lost respect. New legal regulations are a result of fear rather than of self-confidence: the gnostic vision of us as the light side of the force and the internal and foreign challenge as a destructive element whose activity has to be averted, is another attempt to build oppositions that have nothing in common with natural order, where everybody is invited to compete and cooperate at the same time.

Bibliography

Alschen S., 2013, *In the Footsteps of Peter the Great*, [online:] <www1.umassd. edu/euro/2013papers/alschen.pdf> [31 October 2017].

Arendt H., 1973, *The Origins of Totalitarianism*, San Diego – New York – London.

Aristotle, 1998, *Rhetoric. Book 1*, [online:] <www.bocc.ubi.pt/pag/Aristotle-rhetoric.pdf> [31 October 2017].

Bäcker R., 2000, *Międzywojenny eurazjatyzm. Od intelektualnej kontrakulturacji do totalitaryzmu?*, Łódź.

Bäcker R., 2008, *Rozumienie Rosji jako zadanie dla teorii polityki*, „Środkowo-europejskie Studia Polityczne", nr 2, pp. 5–26.

Bäcker R., 2011, *Nietradycyjna teoria polityki*, Toruń.

Badcock S., 2008, *The Russian Revolution: Broadening Understandings of 1917*, "History Compass" 6(1), pp. 243–262, doi: 10.1111/j.1478-0542.2007. 00485.x.

Bamyeh M. A., 2013, *Anarchist Method, Liberal Intention, Authoritarian Lesson: The Arab Spring between Three Enlightenments*, "Constellations" 20(2), pp. 188–202, doi: 10.1111/cons.12031.

Bassin M., Richardson P., Kolosov V., Clowes E. W., Agnew J., Plokhy S., 2017, *1917–2017: The Geopolitical Legacy of the Russian Revolution*, "Geopolitics" 22(3), pp. 1–28, doi: 10.1080/14650045.2017.1308107.

Besançon A., 1981, *The Rise of the Gulag: Intellectual Origins of Leninism*, New York.

Beyrau D., 2015, *Brutalization Revisited: The Case of Russia*, "Journal of Contemporary History" 50(1), pp. 15–37, doi: 10.1177/0022009 414542535.

Bieleń S., 2014, Szanse modernizacji na tle osobliwości rosyjskiej polityki, [in:] S. Bieleń, A. Skrzypek (eds.), *Bariery modernizacji Rosji*, Warszawa.

Blau P. M., 1963, *Critical Remarks on Weber's Theory of Authority*, "The American Political Science Review" 57(2), pp. 305–316.

Bochenski J. M., 1963, *Soviet Russian Dialectical Materialism*, Dodrecht.

Bosiacki A., 1997, *The Origins of Bolshevik Totalitarianism, Lenin's Concept of Law*, "Studia Iuridica" XXXV, pp. 15–42 (in Polish).

Bosiacki A., 2012, *Utopia – władza – prawo. Doktryna i koncepcje prawne bolszewickiej Rosji, 1917-1921*, 2nd ed., Warsaw.

Braithwaite J., Braithwaite V., Cookson M., Dunn L., 2010, *Anomie and Violence: Non-truth and Reconciliation in Indonesian Peacebuilding*, Canberra.

Buckley W. F., Jr., 2007, *Cancel Your Own Goddam Subscription: Notes & Asides from National Review*, New York.

Chaadaev P., 1829, *First Philosophical Letter, Documents in Russian History*, [online:] <http://academic.shu.edu/russianhistory/index.php/Petr_Chaa daev,_First_Philosophical_Letter> [31 October 2017].

Chase Ch. W., 2015, *Square Gnosis, Beat Eros: Alan Watts and the Occultism of Aquarian Religion*, "Self & Society: An International Journal for Humanistic Psychology" 43(4), pp. 322–334, doi: 10.1080/03060497.2016.1142259.

Coalson R., 2013, *Russia's Aleksei Navalny: Hope of the Nation – Or the Nationalists?*, [online:] <https://www.rferl.org/a/russia-navalny-nationa listfears/25059277.html> [25 October 2017].

Court A., 2008, *Hannah Arendt's Response to the Crisis of her Times*, Amsterdam.

Cracraft J., 2010, *The Russian Empire as Cultural Construct*, "Journal of The Historical Society" 10(2), pp. 167–188, doi: 10.1111/j.1540 5923.2010.00297.x.

Dalferth I. U., 2004, The Resurrection: The Grammar of 'Raised', [in:] D. Z. Phillips, M. von der Ruhr (eds.), *Biblical Concepts and Our World*, Basingstoke – New York, pp. 190–208.

Danilevsky N. Y., 2013, *Russia and Europe: the Slavic World's Political and Cultural Relations with the Germanic-Roman West*, Bloomington (first published in "Zvezda" 1868/1869).

Đilas M., 1957, *The New Class: An Analysis of the Communist System*, San Diego.

Dubas A., 2008, *The Menace of the "Brown" Russia: Ethnically Motivated Xenophobia – Symptoms, Causes and Prospects for the Future*, Warsaw.

Dudin M. N., 2014, *The Development of Russia's Economy in the Face of Economic Sanctions: National Interests and Security*, "National Interests Priorities and Safety" 43(280), pp. 2–11.

Fülöp-Miller R., 2011, *Franquism as Authoritarianism: Juan Linz and His Critics*, "Politics, Religion & Ideology" 12(1), pp. 27–50, doi: 10.1080/21567689.2011.564398.

Gallopin G. G., 2009, *Beyond Perestroyka: Axiology and the New Russian Entrepreneurs*, Amsterdam.

Gerschewski J., 2016, Do Ideocracies Constitute a Distinct Subtype of Autocratic Regimes?, [in:] U. Backes, S. Kailitz (eds.), *Ideocracies in Comparison: Legitimation – Co-optation – Repression*, London – New York, pp. 88–105.

Gogin S., 2012, *Homo Sovieticus: 20 Years After the End of the Soviet Union*, "Russian Analytical Digest" 109.

Goldman L., 1971, Reflections on History and Class Consciousness, [in:] I. Meszaros (ed.), *Aspects of History and Class Consciousness*, London.

Goldman W. Z., 1983, *Women, the State and Revolution. Soviet Family Policy and Social Life 1917–1936*, Cambridge.

Gray P. W., 2014, *Vanguards, Sacralisation of Politics, and Totalitarianism: Category-based Epistemology and Political Religion*, "Politics, Religion & Ideology" 15(4), pp. 521–540, doi: 10.1080/21567689.2014.957686.

Grelet G., Smith A. P., 2014, *Proletarian Gnosis*, "Angelaki: Journal of the Theoretical Humanities" 19(2), pp. 93–98, doi: 10.1080/0969725X.2014. 950865.

Grigas A., 2016, *Beyond Crimea: The New Russian Empire*, New Haven – London.

Hearst D., 1999, *Russian Neo-Nazi Stabs Prominent Jew*, "The Guardian", [online:] <https://www.theguardian.com/world/1999/jul/14/davidhearst>.

Hechter M., 2000, *Containing Nationalism*, Oxford – New York.

Herberstein S., 1557, *Moscovia der Hauptstat in Reissen*, Wien, [online:] <www. zum.de/Faecher/Materialien/bosch/russisch/herberstein.pdf> [31 October 2017].

Heydari A., Davoudi I., Teymoori A., 2011, *Revising the Assessment of Feeling of Anomie: Presenting a Multidimensional Scale*, "Procedia – Social and Behavioral Sciences" 30, pp. 1086–1090, doi: 10.1016/j.sbspro. 2011.10.212.

Hickey M. C., 2011, *Competing Voices from the Russian Revolution*, Santa Barbara, CA.

Hobbes T., 1651, *Leviathan*, [online:] <https://www.gutenberg.org/ files/3207/3207-h/3207-h.htm#link2H_4_0113> [31 October 2017].

Hoppe H. H., 2001, *Democracy: The God that Failed: The Economics & Politics of Monarchy, Democracy & Natural Order*, New Brunswick – London.

Hosking G., 2001, *Russia and the Russians: A History*, Cambridge, Mass.

Hotam Y., 2007, *Gnosis and Modernity – A Postwar German Intellectual Debate on Secularisation, Religion and 'Overcoming' the Past*, "Totalitarian Movements and Political Religions" 8(3–4), pp. 591–608.

Jonas H., 1952, *Gnosticism and Modern Nihilism*, "Social Research" 19(4), pp. 430–452.

Kumar K., 2015, *Nationalism and Revolution: Friends or Foes?*, "Nations and Nationalism" 21(4), pp. 589–608, doi: 10.1111/nana.12135.

Laqueur W., 1993, *Black Hundred: The Rise of the Extreme Right in Russia*, "The American Journal of Comparative Law" 41(4).

Laruelle M., 2014, *Alexei Navalny and Challenges in Reconciling "Nationalism" and "Liberalism"*, "Post-Soviet Affairs" 30(4), pp. 276–297.

Laruelle M., 2009, *Russian Nationalism and the National Reassertion of Russia*, Abingdon.

Laruelle M., 2016, *How Islam Will Change Russia*, The Jamestown Foundation, [online:] <https://jamestown.org/program/marlene-laruelle-how-islam-will-change-russia/> [25 October 2017].

Lenin V., 1972, Critical Remarks on the National Question, [in:] V. Lenin, *Collected Works*, Vol. 20, Moscow, pp. 17–21.

Lenin V., 1983, Who Are the "Friends of the people" and How Are They Fighting against Social Democrats, [in:] V. Lenin, *Collected Works*, Vol. 1, Warsaw.

Lenin V., 1986a, [in:] V. Lenin, *Collected Works*, Vol. 17, Warsaw.

Lenin V., 1986b, [in:] V. Lenin, *Collected Works*, Vol. 21, Warsaw.

Lenin V., 1987a, [in:] V. Lenin, *Collected Works*, Vol. 24, Warsaw.

Lenin V., 1987b, The End of the 2nd International, [in:] V. Lenin, *Collected Works*, Vol. 26, Warsaw.

Lohr E., 2003, *Nationalizing the Russian Empire. The Campaign against Enemy Aliens during World War I*, Cambridge, Mass.

Löwy M., 1976, *Marxism and the National Question*, "New Left Review" I/96.

MacMaster, 1967, *Danilevsky: A Russian Totalitarian Philosopher*, Cambridge, Mass.

Mau V., 2015, *The Crisis Which Is Not To Be Missed (Кризис, который нельзя упустить)*, Kommersant, pp. 7–19, [online:] <https://www.kommersant.ru/doc/2683949>.

Meliantsev V. A., 2004, *Russia's Comparative Economic Development in the Long Run*, "Social Evolution & History" 3(1), pp. 106–136.

Michael-Matsas S., 2016, *A Hundred Years after the 1917 October Revolution: Imperialism, War, and Revolution Today*, "Journal of Socialist Theory" 44(4), pp. 419–434, doi: 10.1080/03017605.2016.1236484.

Miley T. J., 1965, *The Mind and Face of Bolshevism*, New York.

Mironov B. N., 2015, *The Russian Revolution of 1917 as a By-Product of Modernization*, "Russian Social Science Review" 56(1), pp. 79–95, doi: 10.1080/10611428.2015.1018751.

Mostafa G., 2013, *The Concept of "Eurasia": Kazakhstan's Eurasian Policy and Its Implications*, "Journal of Eurasian Studies" 4(2), pp. 160–170.

Mulholland M., 2017, *Revolution and the Whip of Reaction: Technicians of Power and the Dialectic of Radicalisation*, "Journal of Historical Sociology" 30(2), pp. 369–402, doi: 10.1111/johs.12118.

Nahirny V., 1983, *The Russian Intelligentsia: From Torment to Silence*, New Brunswick – London.

O'Kane R. H. T., 2015, *Revolutions, Revolts and Protest Movements: Focusing on Violence and Transnational Action*, "Political Studies Review" 13(3), pp. 317–328, doi: 10.1111/1478-9302.12031.

Panov P., 2010, *Nation-building in Post-Soviet Russia: What Kind of Nationalism Is Produced by the Kremlin?*, "Journal of Eurasian Studies" 1, pp. 85–94.

Pellicani L., 2003, *Revolutionary Apocalypse: Ideological Roots of Terrorism*, London – Westport, Conn.

Pipes R., 1994, *The Russian Revolution*, Warsaw.

President of Russia, 2008, *Statement by President of Russia Dmitry Medvedev*, [online:] <http://en.kremlin.ru/events/president/transcripts/1222> [10 September 2017].

President of Russia, 2014, *Address by President of the Russian Federation*, [online:] <http://en.kremlin.ru/events/president/news/20603> [10 September 2017] .

Radkey O. H., 1950, *Russia Goes to the Polls. The Election to the Russian Constituent Assembly of 1917*, Cambridge, Mass.

Rak J., 2015a, *A Typology of Cultural Attitudes as a Device Describing Political Thought of the Populations Influenced by Globalization*, "Anthropological Notebooks" 21(2), pp. 55–70.

Rak J., 2015b, *Toward a New Typology of Revitalistic Attitudes*, "Filosofija. Sociologija" 26(2), pp. 122–128.

Rak J., 2016, *Contra-Acculturative Thought as the Source of Political Violence*, "Terrorism and Political Violence" 28(2), pp. 363–382.

Rak J., 2017, Siatka typologiczna mitów jako narzędzie do badania myśli politycznej, [in:] J. Marszałek-Kawa, K. Kakareko (eds.), *Azjatyckie pogranicza kultury i polityki*, Toruń, pp. 191–226.

Reisigl M., Wodak R., 2001, *Discourse and Discrimination: Rhetorics of Racism and Antisemitism*, London.

Rendle M., Lively A., 2017, *Inspiring a 'Fourth Revolution'? The Modern Revolutionary Tradition and the Problems Surrounding the Commemoration of 1917 in 2017 in Russia*, "Historical Research" 90(247), pp. 230–249, doi: 10.1111/1468-2281.12177.

Rendle M., Retish A. B., 2017, *The 'Lessons' of 1917*, "Revolutionary Russia" 30(1), pp. 1–5, doi: 10.1080/09546545.2017.1323380.

Rendle M., 2005, *The Symbolic Revolution: The Russian Nobility and February 1917*, "Revolutionary Russia" 18(1), pp. 23–46, doi: 10.1080/09546540500091076.

Riegel K.-G., 2007, Marxism-Leninism as political religion, [in:] H. Maier, M. Schäfer (eds.), *Totalitarianism and Political Religions. Volume II: Concepts for the Comparison of Dictatorships*, London – New York, pp. 61–112.

Sargeant E., 1997, *Reappraisal of the Russian Revolution of 1917 in Contemporary Russian Historiography*, "Revolutionary Russia" 10(1), pp. 35–54, doi: 10.1080/09546549708575662.

Sebag Montefiore S., 2007, *Young Stalin*, London.

Shahzad F., 2014, *The Discourse of Fear: Effects of the War on Terror on Canadian University Students*, "American Review of Canadian Studies" 44(4), pp. 467–482, doi: 10.1080/02722011.2014.976232.

Smith A. P., 2014, *Against Tradition to Liberate Tradition: Weaponized Apophaticism and Gnostic Refusal*, "Angelaki: Journal of the Theoretical Humanities" 19(2), pp. 145–159, doi: 10.1080/0969725X.2014.950870.

Snyder L., 1984, *Macro-Nationalisms: A History of the Pan-Movements*, Westport, Conn.

Solzhenitsyn A., 1990, *The Gulag Archipelago 1918-1956*, Warsaw.

Spetzler C. S., Stael Von Holstein C. A., 1975, *Encoding in Decision Analysis*, "Management Science" 22(3), pp. 340–358.

Stalin J., 1945, *Mastering Bolshevism*, New York (originally published in Russian in 1937).

Statdata, 2017, Национальный состав России, [online:] <http://www.statdata.ru/nacionalnyj-sostav-rossii>.

Tanter R., Midlarsky M., 1967, *A Theory of Revolution*, "Conflict Resolution" XI(3), pp. 264–280.

The National-Bolshevik Party website, 2007 (archive), [online:] <https://web.archive.org/web/20070501182900/http://eng.nbp-info.ru:80/cat19/index.html> [25 October 2017].

The Russian Primary Chronicle. Laurentian Text, 1953, transl. and eds. S. Hazzard Cross, O. P. Scherbovitz-Wetzor, Cambridge, Mass.

Thorup M., 2015, *The Total Enemy: Six Chapters of a Violent Idea*, Eugene.

Tidmarsh K., 1993, *Russia's Work Ethic*, "Foreign Affairs", [online:] <https://www.foreignaffairs.com/articles/russian-federation/1993-03-01/russias-work-ethic> [25 October 2017].

Tipaldou S., 2015, *Russia's Nationalist-Patriotic Opposition: The Shifting Politics of Right-Wing Convention in Post Communist Transition*, [online:] https://ddd.uab.cat/pub/tesis/2015/hdl_10803_308508/st1de1.pdf.

Toynbee A., 1939, *The Study of History*, Vol. V: *The Disintegration of Civilizations*, London.

Unwalla Ph., 2015, *Nationalism and Revolution*, "Nations and Nationalism" 21(4), pp. 279–288.

Uvarov S. S., 1832, *A Letter to Nicholas I*, [online:] <http://samoderjavie.ru/uvarov> [25 October 2017].

Varshizky A., 2012, *Alfred Rosenberg: The Nazi Weltanschauung as Modern Gnosis*, "Politics, Religion & Ideology" 13(3), pp. 311–331, doi: 10.1080/21567689.2012.69897.

Voegelin E., 1952, *Gnostische Politik*, "Merkur" 6(4), pp. 301–317.

Voegelin E., 1987, *The New Science of Politics: An Introduction*, Chicago–London.

Voegelin E., 1997, *Science, Politics and Gnosticism: Two Essays*, Washington, D.C.

Voegelin E., 2000, Man in Society and History (1964), [in:] E. Sandoz (ed.), *The Collected Works of Eric Voegelin. Volume 11. Published Essays 1953–1965*, Columbia–London, pp. 191–206.

von Hayek F. A., 1981, Kinds of Order in Society, [in:] R. Raico (ed.), *New Individualist Review*, introd. M. Friedman, Indianapolis, [online:] <http://oll.libertyfund.org/pages/hayek-on-kinds-of-order-in-society> [31 October 2017].

Walicki A., 1975, *The Slavophile Controversy*, Oxford.

Walicki A., 1995, *Filozofia prawa rosyjskiego liberalizmu (Philosophy of Law by the Russian Liberalism)*, Warsaw.

Wallerstein I., 1998, *Utopistics. Or, Historical Choices of the Twenty-First Century*, New York.

Wolfe B. D., 2017, *An Ideology in Power: Reflections on the Russian Revolution*, London, [online:] <https://books.google.pl/books?id=tEUlDgAAQBAJ&pg=PT89&lpg=PT89&dq=rob+what+has+been+robbed+expropriation&source=bl&ots=BdOizBLdR9&sig=f2FBUTeCb8VLcKxQMBWogc1pD_w&hl=pl&sa=X&ved=0ahUKEwi_5aG11JLXAhXBXhoKHQBTBrEQ6AEIKjAA#v=onepage&q=rob%20what%20has%20been%20robbed%20expropriation&f=false> [31 October 2017].

Wood A., 2003, *The Origins of the Russian Revolution, 1861-1917*, London – New York.

World Bank, 2015, *Russia Economic Report. The Dawn of a New Economic Era?*, [online:]<https://openknowledge.worldbank.org/bitstream/handle/10986/21781/956970NWP00PUB0B0WB0RER0No0330FINAL.pdf?sequence=1&isAllowed=y>.

World Bank, 2017, *Russia Economic Report. From Recession to Recovery*, [online:] <https://openknowledge.worldbank.org/bitstream/handle/10986 /27522/116237-WP-P161778-PUBLIC-RERengforweb.pdf?sequence= 1&isAllowed=y>.

ZNAK, 2016, *Интолерантность. «Левада-центр»: более половины россиян симпатизируют идее «Россия – для русских»*, [online:] <https:// www.znak.com/2016-10-11/levada_centr_bolee_poloviny_rossiyan_ simpatiziruyut_idee_rossiya_dlya_russkih> [31 October 2017].

Агентство Русской Информации, 2006, *Итоги Русского Марша Ч 1: Сколько нас было?*, [online:] <https://ari.ru/ari/2006/11/06/itogi-russkogo-marsha-ch-1-skolko-nas-bylo> [31 October 2017].

Блум М. И., 1965, *П. И. Стучка об уголовном и исправительно-трудовом праве*, [в:] *О теоретическом наследии П. И. Стучки в советской правовой науке*, Рига.

Вишневский А., 2016, *«Россия навсегда упустила свой демографический шанс». Демограф Анатолий Вишневский о тяжелом наследии и угрозах для населения России*, беседовал Андрей Мозжухин, [online:] <https:// lenta.ru/articles/2016/10/06/vishnevsky/>.

Габуев А., 2008, *Эдуард Кокойты: мы там практически выровняли все*, "Коммерсантъ" 3961(144), p. 7.

Гойхбарг А. Г., 1918, *Пролетарская революция и гражданское право*, "Пролетарская революция и право", № 1., с. 17.

Гойхбарг А. Г., 1919, *Пролетариат и право. Сборник статей*, Москва.

Гойхбарг А. Г., 1921, *Советское земельное право*, Москва.

Гумилев Л. Н., 2002, *От Руси к России*, Москва.

Данишевский К. Х., 1920, *Революционные военные трибуналы*, Москва.

Декрет об отмене права частной собственности на недвижимость в городах, принятый на заседании Президиума Всероссийского Центрального Исполнительного Комитета 20 августа 1918 г., [в:] *Собрание узаконений и распоряжений рабочего и крестьянского правительства (СУиРРиКП)*, 1918.

Декреты Советской власти, 1964, Москва.

Демоскоп Weekly, 2017, *Первая всеобщая перепись населения Российской Империи 1897 г. Распределение населения по вероисповеданиям и регионам*, "Демоскоп" 741–742, [online:] <http://www.demoscope.ru/weekly/ ssp/rus_rel_97.php?reg=0> [31 October 2017].

Дугин А., 1998, *Основы геополитики: геополитическое будущее России*, Москва.

Еженедельник Чрезвычайных Комиссий по борьбе с контрреволюцией и спекуляцией, 1918, No. 1.

Из-под глыб, 1974, Collection, Paris.

Калашников М., 2014, *Новая инквизиция: кто мешает русскому прорыву?*, Москва.

Коммерсант, 2008, *Сколько членов у российских партий. Вычислительный центр*, [online:] <https://www.kommersant.ru/doc/886287> [31 October 2017].

Лабутова Т., 1990, *Ежегодник Большой советской энциклопедии*, "вып" 34, Москва, pp. 007–011.

Лацис М.И., 1921, *Чрезвычайные комиссии по борьбе с контрреволюцией*, Москва.

Левада-Центр, 2009, *Россия для русских или для всех россиян?*, [online:] <https://www.levada.ru/2009/12/06/rossiya-dlya-russkih-ili-dlya-vseh-rossiyan/> [31 October 2017].

Левада-Центр, 2014, *Почему россияне несчастны?*, [online:] <https://www.levada.ru/2014/10/02/pochemu-rossiyane-neschastny/> [25 October 2017].

Михайлов А., 2016, *Интервью с одним из первых организаторов Русского Марша Алексеем Михайловым*, Русский марш, [online:] <http://rmarsh.info/novosti/interv-yu-s-odnim-iz-pervy-h-organizatorov-russkogo-marsha-alekseem-mihajlovy-m.html> [31 October 2017].

Москва III Рим, 2009, *По официальным данным население России в 2009 г., сократилось на 225 тысяч человек*, [online:] <http://3rm.info/main/1207-po-oficialnym-dannym-naselenie-rossii-v-2009-g.html> [31 October 2017].

Орлова И. В., Соколова Т. Д., 2017, *Роль и функции общественных советов в повышении эффективности деятельности региональных органов государственной власти*, "RUDN Journal of Sociology" 17(1), [online:] <http://journals.rudn.ru/sociology/article/view/15462/14203>.

Пальцев А. И., 2011, *Системообразующие ценности евразийской (российской) цивилизации*, "Власть", № 4, pp. 42–44.

Пионтковский А., 2011, *Третийпуть к рабству*, Москва.

Правозащитный центр "Мемориал", 2014, *Манежное дело*, [online:] <https://memohrc.org/ru/special-projects/manezhnoe-delo-0>.

Президент России, 2008, *Дмитрий Медведев выступил с заявлением в связи с признанием независимости Южной Осетии и Абхазии*, [online:] <http://kremlin.ru/events/president/news/1223> [10 September 2017].

Президент России, 2014, *Обращение Президента Российской Федерации*, [online:] <http://kremlin.ru/events/president/news/20603> [10 September 2017].

Программа русской социал-демократической рабочей партии, 1917, [в:] *Сборник программ русских политических партий. Издание новое с изменениями и дополнениями последних партийных съездов*, Петроград.

Реальное Время, 2017, *Конец демографического чуда: в 2017 году в России началась убыль населения*, [online:] <https://realnoevremya.ru/analytics/78260-v-2017-godu-v-rossii-nachalas-ubyl-naseleniya> [31 October 2017].

Руководящие начала по уголовному праву РСФСР, 1919.

Русский марш, 2017, *Кратко о Русском Марше*, [online:] <http://rmarsh.info/news14/kratko-o-russkom-marshe.html> [31 October 2017].

Савельев А., 2005, *О необходимости и возможности национальной революции в России. Доклад на Санкт-Петербургском патриотическом форуме, 27 октября 2005 года*, [online:] <http://savelev.ru/article/show/?id=287&t=1> [31 October 2017].

Сергеев С. М., 2017a, *Русская нация или Рассказ об истории ее отсутствия: история русского народа, на плечах которого держались все инкарнации Государства российского: Московского царства, Российской империи, Советского Союза — и держится ныне Российская Федерация*, Москва.

Сергеев С. М., 2017b, *Русская нация. Национализм и его враги*, Москва.

Смирнов Н., Портнов В. В., Славин М. М., 1990, *Становление правосудия Советской России (1917-1922 гг.)*, Москва.

Собрание узаконений и распоряжений рабочего и крестьянского правительства (СУиРРиКП), 1917/1918.

Солженицын А. И., 1974, *Письмо вождям Советского Союза*, Paris.

Солженицын А. И., 1978, *Речь в Гарварде на ассамблее выпускников университета*, [online:] <http://antology.igrunov.ru/authors/solzh/1121759601.html> [31 October 2017].

Солженицын А. И., 1990, *Как нам обустроить Россию*, [online:] <http://lib.ru/PROZA/SOLZHENICYN/s_kak_1990.txt> [31 October 2017].

Солженицын А. И., 1998, *Россия в обвале*, [online:] <http://www.rodon.org/sai/rvo.htm#a30> [31 October 2017].

Соловей Т., Соловей В., 2011, *Несостоявшаяся революция*, Москва.

Стучка П. И., 1917a, *На почве закона или на почве революции*, "Правда" № 48.

Стучка П. И., 1917b, *Классовый или демократический суд?*, "Правда" № 85.

Стучка П. И., 1918, *Народный суд в вопросах и ответах*, Москва.

Стучка П. И., 1964, *Избранные произведения по марксистско-ленинской теории права*, Рига.

Тренин Д., 2012, *Post-imperium*, Москва.

Тютчев Ф. И., 2013, *Россия и Революция*, Москва, [online:] <http://feb-web.ru/feb/tyutchev/texts/p06/tu3-144-.htm?cmd=2> [25 October 2017] (originally published in French in 1848).

Федеральная служба государственной статистики, 2012, Социально-демографический образ России по итогам всероссийской переписи населения 2010 года, Москва.

Федеральный закон от 25 июля 2002 г. N 114-ФЗ "О противодействии экстремистской деятельности", 2002, [online:] <https://rg.ru/2002/07/30/extremizm-dok.html> [31 October 2017].

Царский Путь. Русский Оперативный Журнал, 2017, *Россия стабильно вымирает*, [online:] <http://opervzakone.livejournal.com/312311.html> [31 October 2017].

Чернов В., 1924, *Ленин*, "Воля России" 3, pp. 30–36.

Шафаревич И. Р., 1977, *Социализм как явление мировой истории*, Paris.

Шафаревич И. Р., 1988, *Русофобия*, München.

Шафаревич И. Р., 2005, *Трехтысячелетняя загадка*, Москва.

Широпаев А., 2001, *Тюрьма народа*, Москва.

Index of Names

About the Authors

ADAM BOSIACKI – Professor of Legal Sciences at the University of Warsaw, Faculty of Law and Administration. Director of the Institute of Sciences on State and Law, Chair of the History of Political and Legal Doctrines. His academic activity concerns the issues of Russian and Soviet history, the problems of Central and Eastern European law, the history of administration of local and corporative character, the history of legal thought (especially modern), comparative law (mainly public), and the history of science. The author of several monographs and several dozen articles; scholarly editor of the series "Classics of Legal Thought".

JOACHIM DIEC – Professor of Social Sciences at Jagiellonian University in Kraków, Chair in Eurasian Area Studies. Main fields of research: Russian political doctrines, Russia and Eurasia in international relations. Major publications: *Cywilizacje bez okien* (Civilizations Without Windows), Kraków 2002; *Konserwatywny nacjonalizm* (Conservative nationalism), Kraków 2013, *Geostrategiczny wybór Rosji u zarania trzeciego tysiąclecia*, T. 1: *Doktryna rosyjskiej polityki zagranicznej. Partnerzy najbliżsi i najdalsi* (Russia's Geostrategic Choice at the Dawn of the Third Millennium, Vol. 1: The Doctrine of Russia's Foreign Policy. The Closest and the Furthest Partners), Kraków 2015.

IVAN FOMIN – candidate of political sciences; research fellow at Immanuel Kant Baltic Federal University (Kaliningrad); associate professor at the National Research University – Higher School of Economics, Faculty of Social Sciences; research fellow at the INION institute (Moscow). Main fields of research: semiotics, political discourse analysis, secessionism, post-Soviet conflicts. Major publications: *Образы Южной Осетии и Косова в российском внешнеполитическом дискурсе* (Images of South Ossetia and Kosovo in Russian in the Discourse of Russian Foreign Policy), *Полития* (Politeia), 2014, N 2; *Зачем семиотика политологам?* (What Can Semiotics Contribute to Political Science?), *Политическая наука* (Political Science (RU)), 2016, N 3.

Lyudmila Ilyicheva – Doctor of Politics, Director of Center for Public Private Partnership, The Russian Presidential Academy of National Economy and Public Administration.

Joanna Rak – PhD, assistant professor at the Chair of Political Culture at the Faculty of Political Science and Journalism, Adam Mickiewicz University in Poznań. In 2016 and 2017 a visiting researcher at CEU San Pablo University in Madrid. Research interests: cultures of political violence, dynamics of radicalization, anti-austerity movements, political epistemic apparatuses, social mobilization, and cultural security. Major publications: *Contra--Acculturative Thought as the Source of Political Violence*, "Terrorism and Political Violence" 2016, Vol. 28, No. 2; *A Typology of Cultural Attitudes as a Device Describing Political Thought of the Populations Influenced by Globalisation*, "Anthropological Notebooks" 2015, Vol. 21, No. 2; *Toward a New Typology of Revitalistic Attitudes*, "Filosofija. Sociologija" 2015, Vol. 26, No. 2. E-mail: joanna.rak@amu.edu.pl.

W serii *Rosja wczoraj, dziś i jutro. Polityka - kultura - religia* pod redakcją Mieczysława Smolenia, Joachima Dieca i Anny Jach ukazały się:

1. Anna Jach, *Rosja 1991-1993. Walka o kształt ustrojowy państwa*, 2011.
2. *Rozpad ZSRR i jego konsekwencje dla Europy i świata*, cz. 1: *Federacja Rosyjska*, red. Anna Jach, 2011.
3. *Rozpad ZSRR i jego konsekwencje dla Europy i świata*, cz. 2: *Wspólnota Niepodległych Państw*, red. Mieczysław Smoleń i Michał Lubina, 2011.
4. *Rozpad ZSRR i jego konsekwencje dla Europy i świata*, cz. 3: *Kontekst międzynarodowy*, red. Joachim Diec, 2011.
5. *Rozpad ZSRR i jego konsekwencje dla Europy i świata*, cz. 4: *Reinterpretacja po dwudziestu latach*, red. Anna Jach i Michał Kuryłowicz, 2012.
6. Olga Nadskakuła, *Kategorie „swój" i „obcy" w rosyjskim myśleniu politycznym*, 2013.
7. Joachim Diec, *Konserwatywny nacjonalizm. Studium doktryny w świetle myśli politycznej Igora Szafariewicza*, 2013.
8. *Rosyjskie siły zbrojne. Aspekty wewnętrzne i kontekst polski*, red. Anna Jach, 2013.
9. Дмитрий Романовский, *Антоний Храповицкий. философия, богословие, культура*, 2013.
10. Dymitr Romanowski, *Trzeci Rzym. Rozwój rosyjskiej idei imperialnej*, 2013.
11. *Ценности в политике. Опыт Польши и России*, ред. Богдан Шляхта, Анна Ях, 2013.
12. Anna Kadykało, *Dzieciństwo jako rosyjski temat kulturowy w XX wieku*, 2014.
13. Małgorzata Flig, *Mitotwórcza funkcja kina i literatury w kulturze stalinowskiej lat 30. XX wieku*, 2014.
14. *Fenomen Rosji - pamięć o przeszłości i perspektywy rozwoju*, cz. 1: *Pamięć o przeszłości w idei i kulturze Rosji*, red. Martyna Kowalska i Michał Kuryłowicz, 2014.
15. *Fenomen Rosji - pamięć o przeszłości i perspektywy rozwoju*, cz. 2: *Kontekst polityczny i gospodarczy*, red. Joachim Diec i Anna Jach, 2014.
16. *Fenomen Rosji - pamięć o przeszłości i perspektywy rozwoju*, cz. 3: *Na wschód od linii Curzona. Księga Jubileuszowa dedykowana Profesorowi Mieczysławowi Smoleniowi*, red. Renata Król-Mazur i Michał Lubina, 2014.
17. Elżbieta Żak, *Mieszkańcy rosyjskiej świadomości zbiorowej XX i XXI wieku. Bohater kryminałów Aleksandry Marininej i Borysa Akunina*, 2014.
18. Michał Lubina, *Niedźwiedź w cieniu smoka. Rosja-Chiny 1991-2014*, 2015.
19. Michał Kuryłowicz, *Polityka zagraniczna Uzbekistanu wobec Rosji*, 2015.
20. Marta Lechowska, *Teatr misteryjny w kulturze Rosyjskiej*, 2015.

21. *Rewolucja rosyjska. Spuścizna. „Implementacje strategii" zmiany*, red. Anna Jach, 2017.
22. *Rewolucja rosyjska. Spuścizna. Międzynarodowe echa rewolucji*, red. Michał Kuryłowicz, 2017.